there is nothing to fear in this moment, and
this is the only real moment there is

The Earth House

JEANNE DUPRAU

The
Earth
House

Fawcett Columbine • New York

A Fawcett Columbine Book
Published by Ballantine Books

This edition published by arrangement with New Chapter Press, Inc.

Library of Congress Catalog Card Number: 92-97331

ISBN: 0-449-90814-3

Cover design by James R. Harris
Author photo by Harriet Craske

Manufactured in the United States of America

First Ballantine Books Edition: June 1993

10 9 8 7 6 5 4 3 2 1

*To the memory of Sylvia Reid
and
to Cheri*

1

Silence

It's night. I see it in my memory as a great black spherical night, pricked with stars, and down at its base, very small and insignificant, shines a gleam of yellow light. It comes from between the flaps of a large army surplus tent, a tent that might once have housed an infirmary or a command post out on some battlefield. Now it's here on a hill in the Sierra Nevadas, the only human structure in the surrounding three hundred and twenty acres of land. It has become, in a transformation that would bemuse its former occupants, the first building of a Zen Buddhist monastery and mountain retreat.

Inside, six people sit in a row at a narrow table that runs along one wall of the tent. We are eating lentil soup, which has been brought from home and warmed up on the Coleman stove, and untoasted French bread, and apple salad. A propane lamp hangs from the beam that supports the tent's peaked roof and sends out a wavering deep gold light. The light casts our shadows onto the canvas in front of us. Mine has a weirdly pointed head because I have put up the hood of my sweatshirt against the cold. The lamp hisses steadily. Moths flutter against it. The sound of my own chewing fills my ears, and between mouthfuls I hear other people's chewing, and their forks tapping against paper plates, and their jackets rustling as they shift position on the bench. These are the only sounds; there is no conversation. Here at this place the rule is silence.

Otherwise, we would surely be talking about our day, which has been full of accomplishment and novelty. We've set up the kitchen at one end of the tent and the meditation hall at the other. For the kitchen we've made this long narrow table and painted it white; we've made counters on which to set the Coleman stove, our jugs of drinking water, our bags of food; we've pounded nails into the top beam of the tent frame and from them we've hung the familiar kitchen implements: vegetable peeler, slotted spoon, measuring cups. For meditation we built two low platforms, one on either side of a narrow aisle, and covered them with scraps of carpet. Our round black meditation cushions sit in a neat row on each platform. In a place with different rules, we'd be reporting how it was to have done all this, exclaiming over the results, assessing our progress, and planning our next steps. Instead, keeping the silence, we just eat.

I am new to it, and I don't entirely understand. Silence seems depressing to me, strange and unfriendly. In my years of hard struggle to become socially correct, I have learned that you don't eat with someone and not talk unless you are mad at each other, or unless you've been married so many years you have nothing left to say. I'm uneasy; my mind flails around. If we can't talk, how are we going to occupy ourselves all evening?

We do the dishes, which means throw our paper plates into the garbage sack and wipe off our forks and knives. We wrap our hands around our cups of tea. Now we sit facing the center of the tent, our legs on the outside of the benches, our backs against the edge of the table. It is the perfect moment for conversation, or for story telling. I do not know what to do with my eyes. I dart looks at the other people. Beside me is Sylvia, my companion. She is looking past her tea at the floor. Steam rises before her face. On the bench beside her are Jennifer, who stares serenely into the air through her round glasses, Phyllis, who is used to silence — she has been a nun for twenty years — and Greg, who must also be content with silence, or he would not be intending to come and live here. And sitting on the red cooler, elbows on her knees, the collar of her black jacket turned up around her face, is the Guide, who of course has no trouble with silence at all. She is the one who ordained the silence. She *likes* it. She drinks her tea peacefully, smiling at the floor.

Beyond the thin canvas of the tent is the huge black night — the sharp stars, the pine and oak trees pitch black against the sky, aloof in their stillness, like tall people who know what night is all about and are not interested in talking to us about it. Since I have no choice, I listen to the sounds the night has to offer: the hoots of an owl, insects batting against the sides of the tent, remote liquid bird calls, and occasionally, from out beyond the boundary of the property, across the fence where the land has been cleared for cow pasture, the hysterical chorus of coyotes, starting with one voice and escalating into a wild frenzy of yipping and howling.

The night is made to get away from, it seems to me. That's why we have lights and fires and houses. That's why we talk to each other at night, to keep ourselves on the manageable human plane.

The cold begins to creep inside my collar and up the legs of my jeans. My tea is almost gone. No one speaks, but I realize that I am not, after all, sitting in a still pool of silence. A tremendous racket is going on inside my head. Music blares — marches, strangely enough, brass bands playing things like "Seventy-Six Trombones" and "Stars and Stripes Forever." The music started up when I was eating my dinner, as accompaniment to the steady beat of my chewing, and it has continued with undiminished force. Laid over the music is an unceasing succession of fretful remarks: "This is strange. I don't like it. I'm cold. It's too dark here. My tea isn't hot enough. It was stupid of me not to have brought a warmer jacket. Why doesn't someone talk? What is Sylvia thinking? Does she like this? I don't see why we need to be so quiet, it doesn't make sense, it's so lonely and so boring, how am I going to stand it here? I am no good at the spiritual life, these other people can do it but not me . . . ." And on and on, with no pauses.

"In silence," the Guide has told us, "it's easier to hear the voices in your head." I've had enough of the voice in my head already. Why should I sit silent up here in the woods at night in order to listen to this endless griping?

But I know why. I have to admit that I know why, though I do so reluctantly. It's why I came to this practice in the first place, why I have taken to sitting in front of a blank wall every day for thirty minutes at a time. Something was awry in my life. There was a dissatisfaction, an undercurrent of discontent that was there all the time, no matter how hard I gathered in friends and possessions and activities.

I went to a therapist, hoping to find out what was wrong with me by scrutinizing my past and my dreams. I thought that eventually all the old buried and petrified stuff of my life would bubble up and explode like lava out of a volcano, and afterward I would be changed. I kept waiting for this to happen. But instead of finding answers I found new questions, I piled up questions more and more thickly around myself, I explained and analyzed everything I had ever done, combing through it for the key to my gloom and anger and discovering instead only new places to look.

In therapy, I talked until I was sick of talking. In meditation I was to be silent and listen. "It's all there," the Guide said, "everything you need to know. Just pay attention, you'll start to see." She told this story to illustrate:

"Suppose you get up one morning to find that the book you were reading the night before is gone. You think you've misplaced it. You look all over the house, but you can't find it. Very puzzling. The next morning, you see when you get up that a lamp is gone from an end table. This is alarming. You check all the doors — they're locked. You check the windows: locked, too. And yet the lamp is gone. The next morning, you discover that the couch has disappeared. Unmistakable — a blank place where it once was. Terrible! You are being robbed! What should you do?

"There are several possible courses. You could call the police. You could call everyone you know who has a key to your house. You could install a burglar alarm system. But the answer that makes the best sense is this: *Stay up all night and watch very carefully.*"

And it's the same with your life, she told us: if something's missing, if you suspect that something is going on that mysteriously robs you of your happiness, the best way to get to the bottom of it is to stay awake. This mountain retreat was to be a place that encouraged staying awake, as the circumstances of ordinary life do not.

....

Our tea is gone. It is nearly eight-thirty. We get up from our bench and file to the other end of the room, where the darkness is deeper. No shoes here; we leave them behind in the kitchen and step onto the carpet in our sock-covered feet. Then the familiar ritual: Stand at the edge of the platform, bow with palms together to the black cushion, the zafu. Turn, bow to each other, to the room. Sit down, swivel around, arrange the hands, fingers overlapping, thumbs touching. Face the canvas of the tent, on which our shadows loom, slanted and wavering. The Guide strikes the tiny brass bowl that is the bell, and the sound hangs thin and clear in the cold air.

We sit, and silence settles in the room like snow. Even the night has grown quiet. No sound comes from beyond the tent now; the darkness has frozen. The silence penetrates like the cold, into the folds of the tent, into the dark space beneath the rafters, into the hollows of the cooking pots and the row of empty shoes — everywhere, except into the brightly lit rumpus room of my mind, where there is ceaseless commotion.

2

The Center, the Guide, and the Land

What I meant to do when I began this writing was tell about what happened to Sylvia and me at the monastery in the mountains — how the place entered our lives and turned them in surprising directions — and tell also about Zen Buddhism as it is practiced there. My book would be two stories, woven together. But it has had to become three. Our path took an unexpected turn, and the new life we embarked on was cut short for Sylvia and deeply changed for me.

Sylvia and I were partners in our exploration of Zen Buddhism, as we had been in other ways for a long time. We had known each other since our teens, and we had lived together in Sylvia's suburban house since our mid-thirties. Our lives were calm and unremarkable. I spent my weekdays in a cubicle at a computer company, writing training materials; Sylvia spent hers in a dentist's office, cleaning the plaque off people's teeth. We had an adequate amount of money and a satisfying number of friends and activities. We were as happy as anyone else.

We had not been searching for a spiritual path — or if we had been, we hadn't known it. Both of us had done a bit of meditation now and then, both of us had read a little about Eastern religions in college courses and felt a mild affinity for them, but we had never been moved to do anything about it. When we heard through friends of a small Zen center in a nearby town, we went there not because we were avid to take up Zen practice, but out of curiosity and some vague inclination to find something deeper than our everyday experience.

When the student is ready, it is said, the teacher will appear. It's as if the student is a magnet, wandering around the world, maybe not even aware of being a magnet needing something to attach to, and the teacher is a piece of steel. When the student wanders into the teacher's presence, there is the clang of steel and magnet coming together. There is no question, no need for debate, no need to weigh the pros and cons of this teacher against another one. This is what happened to Sylvia and me, to both of us at the same time.

I know that spiritual teachers are springing up everywhere, some of them genuine and some quacks; cult leaders and peculiar gurus are described in lurid detail in the newspapers, especially the ones whose followers do something outrageous, like poisoning themselves, or building bomb shelters stocked with machine guns in the wilderness. I don't know about these other teachers, and I am not interested in speculating about them, or in comparing this one with them. I have discovered by now that telling a true spiritual teacher from a huckster is not always easy. You have to look closely, you have to be patient, you have to admit into your criteria of judgment some possibilities that you might not have considered before. The Guide says, "There are no good teachers, only good students." A good student, this means, can learn from anyone, from anything. A good student, a sincere seeker, can learn lessons of great value from a fraud; a poor student will be impervious to the teaching of even the greatest teacher.

The teacher at this Zen center was a woman, no one famous. She hadn't been written up in the newspaper, she was not affiliated with well-known Zen centers. She was a small, compact, ruddy-faced person, dressed in black pants and a black shirt, with short graying hair, radiant energy, and an uninhibited laugh. She talked and talked during the day-long session we went to, and most of what she said I have now forgotten, except for one thing, which I remember because it was what struck Sylvia most of all: "There is nothing to fear," she said. "*Nothing* to fear."

Later Sylvia told me that she could tell from the way the Guide leaned forward and spoke so clearly and steadily that she must know from experience that what she said was true. How there could be nothing to fear in a world full of nuclear bombs, rapists, earthquakes, and incurable diseases we were not at that point sure. But Sylvia, for one, was interested in finding out.

It struck her with particular intensity because she had had a scare a couple of years before: a mole on her shoulder had turned out to be melanoma, a fast-spreading kind of cancer that is almost always fatal. Surgery had removed the mole and a chunk of flesh around it, and the doctors assured her it was very likely they'd got it all. Since then no sign of it had appeared, and the fear had faded somewhat. Still, she had been reminded of her mortality, and this is especially jolting when you are only thirty-eight years old, and when you feel that you have not yet done whatever it is you're meant to do.

Soon after the surgery, Sylvia had a vivid dream. She was climbing a steep mountain, scrambling for a foothold, struggling through darkness. At last she fell to her knees and cried out in great anguish, "How shall I live?" In the years since then she had been looking for the answer, and she felt right away that this teacher and this practice of Zen Buddhist meditation might help her to find it. I remember that we exchanged a look halfway through that first day: This is all right, the look said. This teacher is real.

Not everyone thinks so, of course. The Guide is not everyone's cup of tea. There is the fact that she is a woman, and although a growing number of women teach Zen meditation in America, in many views a *real* teacher must be a man, and a man in possession of an authentic dharma transmission, someone to whom spiritual authority has been handed down by way of an ancient lineage of officially recognized Zen masters. The Guide is not this. She has no official Buddhist credentials and tells people so. She was trained, over five years, at a monastery in the mountains, by a Zen master of great sternness — many people would say harshness. There she learned how to continue with her life, which she had considered ending. She is a fierce and funny and unpredictable leader, with energy so boundless as to be almost terrifying. And she is at the same time a person leading a late-twentieth-century life, indistinguishable on the street from people leading more conventional lives, except that her jeans and sweatshirts are almost always black, and her expression shows none of the deadness, the furrows of chronic anxiety, the dull, distracted look of people whose minds are on their worries.

The Guide does not claim to be an enlightened being. "When people tell you they're enlightened," she says, "you can be pretty sure they're not." She does not claim *not* to be enlightened, either. The subject of who is enlightened and who isn't does not come up. For our purposes, the Guide is someone who is practicing Buddhism, and has been doing so longer and more intensely than we have. She does her practice and passes on what she knows.

And she does it by means of a mixture of Buddhism and psychology, in the kind of group work that is familiar to millions, especially in California. Its familiar form, however, lacks the spiritual dimension that is always present at the Zen Center. Therapy is usually designed to strengthen your ego, to help you adjust to the world; in spiritual training you examine the ego and its devious operations only so that you can recognize it when you see it, so that you can understand how it runs your life. The aim is not to improve the ego, or strengthen it, but to see it clearly so that you can look past it. Sitting in on one of the Center's discussions, you might for a while forget that we are talking about the practice of Zen Buddhism. Words more familiar in psychological circles than religious ones dominate the talk: people speak of their "subpersonalities," parts of their psyche that act as if they were autonomous beings; they talk about ego and projection, belief systems and postures. This is twentieth-century language, the language of psychology and of the personal growth movement. But it isn't watered-down Buddhism, or pop Buddhism; it is a translation that makes Buddhism accessible to modern, Western people.

Sylvia and I started going to the Center once a week, for meditation and discussion. At home afterward, we reviewed what we'd heard. We were accustomed to tackling new concepts with our minds — thinking about them, talking about them, relating them to more familiar ideas. But the concepts of Zen are mysteriously elusive when pursued with the mind. They slip away. You think you understand, you begin to put your understanding into words, but the more you talk the more you realize that somehow you haven't quite got it, or else that what you've got can't possibly be right. You must have heard wrong. What you thought you heard makes no sense. Or does it? Something in you leans toward it, some faint bell sounds in a distant inaccessible part of you, just loudly enough to keep you puzzling, to keep you from giving up.

For months we talked, thought, read, and meditated. For a while, the zeal of new converts fired us. I expounded Zen ideas, as I understood them, to my friends, who, it seemed to me, desperately needed this saving information. Instead of being grateful, they stared at me suspiciously. One of them told me that she had an inclination to hit me over the head with a two-by-four, I was so obnoxiously ardent. This phase passed gradually; it became clear, little by little, that you do not do the practice of Zen with your mind, you do not learn it the way we learned other bodies of knowledge — by studying, memorizing, fitting ideas into familiar logical frameworks. You understand only by doing, and the understanding is something that you cannot necessarily put into words. It is more like learning to ride a bicycle than learning a subject in school: you do not do it by following a set of instructions but by trying again and again to do that which seems impossible, and which you have no idea how to go about, until after a while the way grows in you. You can learn to ride a bicycle, however, in a few days or weeks, and once you've learned it you've got it for good. The practice of Zen takes your whole life, and there is never a point at which you have accomplished it and have nothing more to learn.

We didn't know, when we started at the Center, that this practice was a lifetime endeavor. We didn't know the hard places it would bring us up against. If we had known, we might have set forth with less certainty. As it was, the enthusiasm of the beginner got us a good distance in, and from there it became harder and harder to turn back. As time went by, we edged toward deeper involvement. At home, we cautiously increased our daily meditation time from ten minutes to fifteen, fifteen to twenty. We added Sunday morning meditation at the Center to our regular Monday evenings. We started to feel part of the place rather than visiting outsiders. And so, when the Guide began to talk of buying land in the mountains, we listened as if the plan might have something to do with us.

The land in the mountains, she said, was to be an extension of the practice — a place where you could stay as long as you wanted, away from the distractions of your ordinary life. Retreats and workshops would be held there, and a few people — those who wanted to devote themselves entirely to their spiritual practice — would stay there permanently, leading a monastic life. There would be no charge for anything, and anyone — Buddhist, Christian, undecided — could come.

A real estate agent was found and briefed. She scouted out suitable properties. The Guide and a few others went up to look at them, and after some months a decision was made. The Center became the owner of three hundred and twenty hilly, forested acres. I will call this place Middlefield. That is not its actual name, but it seems an appropriate pseudonym, combining Buddhism (which is known as "the middle way") with nature.

Our purchase of the land caused a stir in the community. I imagine the neighbors thought along these lines: "Zen Buddhists? What are they? Are they going to be swarming up and down our road in weird outfits with ponytails sprouting off their bald heads, and are we going to hear chanting in the middle of the night, and will they be holding huge gatherings of cultists who will drive up and down the road and carve big ruts in it? Will they try to subvert our children?"

But it turned out that the Buddhists were a handful of men and women who bought nails and rope and plywood at the local hardware store, and whose only oddities of appearance were black T-shirts that said "Inner Peace — World Peace" in Chinese characters, and short hair, though not any shorter than plenty of people in other walks of life.

And certainly there was no need to be alarmed about noise. No more noise came from the Center's dusty Toyota truck or station wagon than from anyone else's car on that road. Except for the occasional growl of the chainsaw or bang of a hammer, no noise came from the Center's property at all: no carloads of visitors, no loud parties, no rock festivals. Not even radios, because radios were a violation of the silence.

The monastery is at the top of a long road dotted with houses in various rural styles, some with wide porches and shady trees and a few well-kept horses, others with trailers and car bodies in the front yard. When you have passed these, come over the crest of the hill, and begun to descend the other side, you arrive at an aluminum gate with a sign attached to it that says politely, "Please do not enter unless expected."

Beyond the gate is a long curving dirt road with a series of grassy meadows along it, and beyond the meadows are hills thick with oaks and pines and manzanitas. The road runs from east to west, down the center of the property. To the south, the land slopes upward to a ridge. To the north it descends, and at the bottom of the slope, about half a mile away, is a creek that runs along the back boundary of the land. In summer it's a bed of smooth rocks with tangles of blackberry vines on either side. In winter, in years when rain breaks the drought, the stream can be a torrent that washes out the fragile country road that runs along it.

Where Middlefield's road levels out there is a wide clearing presided over by a tremendous ponderosa pine. You have a feeling of arrival when you get here, though at first there was nothing to arrive at. But it's obviously a *place*, flat and open, and with a view to the west of wave after wave of hills. There is where, a few months later, we set up the tent.

Keep walking down the road, which is roofed like an arbor with arching branches, and you come to a meadow on the left. The trees recede here, and the space between road and woods is grass except for where an oak tree fell years ago; its long gray trunk is decomposing picturesquely, branches pointing at the sky. This is the upper meadow. A few paces farther down, past a thicket of trees, is the lower meadow, a wide open grassy space that turns gold in the summer.

Beyond the lower meadow the land gets drier and rockier. Instead of big trees there are low scrub oaks and toyon bushes and manzanita. At the very end of the road is a fence made of rough posts and barbed wire, and beyond it a vista of cropped, almost treeless hills: the neighboring rancher's pastureland, with black and white cows roaming over it.

This place has a smell, completely distinctive: a weedy, sour, pungent smell made up of oak leaves, woodsmoke, wind off the cow pasture, and sometimes in summer, forest fires. It's a strong deep smell that hits you in the back of the nose — pine pollen, bark, toadstools shoving up through the dirt after a rain, mud and dust. It's the smell of everything slowly, slowly becoming dirt — the leaves that fall off the trees, bodies of bugs and birds, the scat dropped by skunks and coyotes and rabbits and deer, the bark peeling off trunks, the lupine finishing its purple spires and wilting, along with the leaves and stems and petals and tendrils of everything else, falling into decay and giving off that smell of thick, brown, stirring life.

We loved it, both of us. To Sylvia, especially, the place felt like home. She had spent the summers of her childhood at a camp in the California hills surrounded by the same dry yellow grass, pine needles, oak trees, and hot blue sky. I had seen photographs of her there — Sylvia on the tennis court in her sleeveless white shirt, Sylvia sitting straight and easy on horseback, an older Sylvia, grown from camper to counselor, standing with the little girls of her cabin. That camp was her heart place; it appeared over and over in her dreams. For her the land at Middlefield was something found again after a long time lost.

No human beings had ever left much of a trace here except the man who sold it to us — he had put in the roads so that buyers could see what they were getting — and, in earlier centuries, the Indians and goldminers. Nothing permanent, no signs but the arrowheads we find now and then buried in the dirt, and the square-headed nails that turn up corroded with rust.

We too wanted to be here in as traceless a way as possible, like good guests who observe and adapt to the customs of the household. Not that the signs of our presence would be unnoticeable; we would not be pitching bark dwellings in the depths of the forest. We knew we would soon feel the need of more shelter than a tent, more amenities than a campfire and a bush to squat behind. But to begin with, in those very first days, all we left were the tracks of our waffle-soled shoes in the dust of the road.

3

Zen Practice: Hard Work

The day came to erect our first structure — the thirty-foot army tent that would be kitchen and meditation hall. Ten of us gathered in the weedy open area by the big ponderosa pine and waited for instructions. We didn't know how to set up a thirty-foot army tent — we had never done it before. The Guide never had, either, but her way is to assume she can do it and figure it out. Ours is to assume we can't and wait for her to show us.

The first step was to build a frame for the tent out of the two-by-fours that waited in a stack at the side of the clearing. We measured boards, drew pencil lines across them, and cut them with a saw more or less along the pencil lines. We held levels up against the verticals and the horizontals and squinted at the little yellow-green bubble floating in the capsule. We hammered nails into the feet of two-by-fours. *Whang whang*, went the hammers, and more times than not the nail buckled and doubled over like a person struck by a stomachache. So we practiced using the tool called a cat's paw: we jammed its claws under the nailhead and levered up the nail. *Squawk*, it came out of the board, and we tried again.

Board by board, the frame went up. "Are we square?" said the Guide. "Are we good?" The sun beat down on us; we sweated, and dust stuck to the sweat. We hoisted up the roof beam; we nailed the rafters to it; we tacked on diagonal braces to keep the verticals from leaning sideways. And in the late afternoon, there it was, the astonishing result of our efforts: the skeleton of a building, all in the deep yellowish tan of the two-by-fours, sitting solidly on the ground, ready for its skin.

And the skin was an acre of canvas as tough as rhinoceros hide, cracked and leathery and inflexible, smelling like basement storerooms and hot jeep engines. We spread it out over the weeds and lined up around it, and somehow we hauled it over the top of the frame, choking underneath in the suffocating heat and darkness. We lashed the tent on with its ropes, staked it, pulled it tight. And we had a building — a long dim room in which the dust circulated slowly in shafts of sunlight that came in through the slits and rope holes. We gazed on the results of our labors, exhausted and pleased with ourselves.

This was the beginning of the work, a sort of preview or advertising sample. It had the features of much of the work that was to come: it was something we didn't know how to do; it seemed at the outset impossibly difficult, even for someone who *did* know how to do it; it involved lifting heavy objects, enduring extreme temperatures, risking humiliation, and inviting bruises, blisters, and sore muscles.

Hard work is the daily bread of this place. It is necessary on the practical level to keep things going, and on the spiritual level it provides the context for the practice. You work, you meditate, and you watch the gyrations of your mind. No latitude is given for ignorance, or for weakness. On the contrary — the harder the job is, the more trouble and pain it causes you, the better for your spiritual muscles it is.

For each person who was planning to spend a fair amount of time at Middlefield, we would build, the Guide said, a hermitage — a small plywood house with a roof of corrugated tin. To begin with, Greg was to be the monastery's only full-time resident. He was ready to quit his job as a manager at a computer company, divest himself of most of his possessions, leave his apartment, and take up the life of a monk. A few months later, Phyllis and Jennifer would make the same decision. Both were teachers at a Montessori school; Phyllis was also a Catholic nun, but her order was willing to let her make this interesting spiritual experiment.

So as the summer turned into fall, we began building hermitages. I remember a day in November, a very cold day. The sky was low and gray, not with clouds that moved but with a dense stationary overcast. No sun came through at all. The cold seeped in through our layers of clothes and gradually chilled us until our joints moved reluctantly and our noses were pinched and runny. Wearing gloves to keep our hands warm, we worked clumsily — missing nails, dropping hammers. Someone lost her grip on a two-by-four, which toppled over and hit Sylvia on the head.

That day we were making a hermitage floor. The piers had been set, and the beams had been laid across them and nailed down. We were fastening sheets of plywood to the beams. You do this on your hands and knees, pounding in a nail every few inches around the edge of the sheet. My knees were raw. My ears crackled with every whack of the hammer. It started to get dark. Water that had spilled from a bucket onto the ground began to form a crust of ice. Can't we stop now? I said in my head. It's dark! It's freezing! But we worked on until the last minute of light. Then the Guide looked up as though surprised, remarked that it was getting hard to see, and said — almost apologetically, as though we might be disappointed — that we'd better quit. She said this, it seemed to me, a very long time after any sensible person would have called it a day.

I kept forgetting that we weren't there to be sensible people. We were there to learn something that seems to most sensible people highly implausible: that essential well-being does not depend on outer circumstances. "It's not what but how," says the Guide, over and over again. It's not what you do that matters, it's how you do it. You can scrub the outhouse in a haze of joy, and you can eat chocolates in a ritzy hotel with discontent churning through your spirit. The task is to wrench apart the automatic associations: Eat chocolate in ritzy hotel = fun. Scrub outhouse = not fun. To this end, life here is designed to be hard, to give you a chance to answer for yourself the kinds of questions that would never otherwise be posed: Can you be all right pushing a wheelbarrow full of rocks up a steep incline in 105-degree heat? Can you be all right slicing carrots every day for five hundred days in a row? Can you be all right while flies whirl around your head and ticks drop on you from the bushes and poison oak makes a lumpy red path up your arm?

The sensible answer to these questions is No. Of course not. Nasty circumstances cause suffering, that's how it works. Oddly enough, though, most of the people who come to a meditation practice have already discovered that outward circumstances and inward response are not necessarily connected, only they have discovered it in reverse. They have found to their bewilderment that although they have what they had thought were the requirements for happiness — a good job, a partner, some money, a pleasant place to live, various activities to use up leisure time — contentment eludes them. They can't figure this out. It seems, contrary to reason, that pleasant circumstances don't necessarily make you happy.

Once you've seen this, you'd think the corollary would also be clear: that unpleasant circumstances don't necessarily make you miserable. This is harder to understand, though evidence of it is all around.

Here are some circumstances I would call unpleasant, in which I, in my current state of spiritual development, would be likely to feel unhappy: dangling from a peg stuck into the sheer side of a mountain over a thousand-foot drop; spending all day peering into hot car engines; writing books on political theory; walking a tightrope strung between skyscrapers. But people exist who do these things of their own free choice. They are happy doing these things, one assumes, or they would not do them. So misery is not built into these activities, only attached to them from the outside.

Here's another astonishing instance of the same principle. Henry David Thoreau wrote in his journal, on a boat trip from Boston to Portland: "Midnight — head over the boat's side — between sleeping and waking — with glimpses of one or more lights in the vicinity of Cape Ann. Bright moonlight—the effect heightened by seasickness." That Thoreau could even notice the moonlight through his seasickness is marvelous to me. I would have my eyes shut against the hateful world; if I were looking at the water, I'd be willing it to hold still instead of sparkling with all that annoying moonlight. For me, the logic would be inescapable: "I am seasick, therefore I am miserable." Thoreau stops at "I am seasick."

Then there's the story of the strawberry. I read this story many times before it made any sense to me. I didn't get it. I thought the hero of it had simply flipped out, stressed beyond his capacities. The story is the one about the man who for some reason is clinging to the side of a cliff, held up only by a thin root which a mouse is gnawing in two. Down below, waiting ravenously, is a tiger. There is no way out of this predicament. The man will drop in a few seconds and be devoured. But he notices, growing a few inches away, a plump red strawberry. He plucks it and eats it. "How delicious!" he says with delight, seconds before he falls into the tiger's jaws.

Here is someone who has learned about as thoroughly as a person can the implausible truth: that no law of the universe says that one's state of mind must inevitably be governed by the circumstances in which one finds oneself. In the last moment of his life, he understands that he has a choice: he can occupy that moment with terror, or he can occupy it with a strawberry. I suppose it's possible that in the dazzling clarity of that last moment the man becomes enlightened — but I think not. I think it more likely that such an attitude takes long practice — the kind of practice that you go to a place like Middlefield to do.

What we come here for, the Guide tells us, is to find out how we make ourselves suffer. How come we're not like the man with the strawberry, alive to the possibilities of every separate moment? What hinders us?

So we watch ourselves work, and if we watch hard enough we begin to get some inklings. Suppose I am building the frame for the tent. I nail some boards together, and then I realize I've done it wrong and I'm going to have to take them apart. What's involved in putting the boards together is this:

1. Measure the boards
2. Saw them in the correct lengths
3. Place them where they belong and put the level up against them to see if they're right
4. Nail them in

Here's what's involved in taking the boards apart:

1. Wedge the end of the cat's paw under the nail head
2. Wrench the nail out

The first activity has four steps; the second, two. It is not harder than the first. It's the same stuff: you move your muscles, you pound, you lift. Someone from another planet, not understanding what project was going forward, would see that the first task is done with cheerful energy and the second, which looks very much like the first, only quicker and easier, is done with a frown. Person from Another Planet would be mystified. What is the difference?

I have invented the difference. In my imagination, like a huge painting on a museum wall entitled How Things Should Be, is a picture of the finished product: the perfect tent frame. The picture is vivid, and I keep my eyes on it, thinking that what I want to do is create a matching reality, forgetting that what I want to do — or at least what I've *said* I want to do — is to be happy. I can no longer see the work in front of my nose for what it is. My eyes look past it, to a successful completion.

So that's one hindrance: attachment to the results of effort. Here's another one. Let's say I'm digging a hole. Digging holes figured heavily in our time at Middlefield; there were the holes for outhouses, holes for fence posts, holes to plant things in, holes for pipes and wires. Imagine me digging an outhouse hole, which has to be about six feet deep and a couple of feet across. I start with a shovel, but in that hard dry ground, full of rocks, a shovel just makes a powdery dent. So I switch to an iron digging stick, a heavy thick rod with a point on one end and a blade on the other. I lift it in both hands and drive it down into the ground, and it makes a shallow pit and loosens up about a tablespoon of dirt. I loosen up dirt, and chip away at the walls, and the hole gets deeper little by little.

It's killing work. My shoulders ache. On the palms of my hands, blisters rise and fill and break, and the digging stick rubs against the fresh red skin underneath. After a while, only a few seconds of ramming the spike into the ground causes the oxygen to drain from my muscles and a blaze of pain to take its place. Tiny flies hang before my eyes, bobbing and darting, looking for the best way in.

While I work, a commentary proceeds in my head, as if someone in me is worried that I will fail to notice what's going on. It points everything out, like a deranged tour guide. "It's hot!" it screams. "I'm sweaty! This digging stick weighs a ton! Flies are trying to get me! I'm not making any progress! My blisters hurt!" Most likely I would have been aware of these truths without the remarks. The remarks are extra. In themselves, hard digging, sore muscles, flies, and heat do not inevitably add up to misery.

What's happened in a situation like this is that I've split my awareness into two levels: the experience itself — the sensations of heat, fire in the muscles, water streaming down the skin, hands gripping iron — and the commentator who stands away from these sensations and forms opinions about them, focusing most often on what is unsatisfactory and outlining how it should be instead. I am accustomed to listening to the commentator, believing that what she says is the truth about my experience. The commentator tells me that the truth about digging a hole is that it causes misery and that instead of heat and pain we should have cool weather and either unlimited strength or an easier job. But the *real* truth — although I can rarely remember it because I'm listening so hard to the commentator's ringing voice — is that there is no unchanging truth *about* my experience but only my experience itself. Everything *about* it is something my commentator has made up by comparing this experience with her concept of one that would be superior. If I want to be like the man with the strawberry, I must disregard my compelling visions of how things *should be* and allow myself to step without resistance into how things *are*.

It takes practice. You can practice at a monastery or somewhere else. Sylvia and I practiced at the monastery some of the time, and the rest of the time we tried to remember to practice at home. The trouble is, at home you forget that your purpose is to find out how you make yourself suffer. You slip into thinking that the goal is to get to the successful end of whatever project you have in hand. That's the point of a place like Middlefield. It's made explicitly clear there that behind the building and cleaning, the repairing and watering and cooking, only one thing is going on: we are finding out how we make ourselves suffer. The awareness of that one purpose hangs in the air always, and if you forget it, the Guide reminds you. "When we get this place built," she says, "we'll have to sell the property and move somewhere else so we can start all over again." She laughs, but you know she would do it in a second.

4

Buying Property

Possibly, said the Guide, a few Center people might consider buying pieces of this new property. This would help the Center finance the purchase and also be a way for people to acquire country property at a reasonable rate and adjacent to quiet neighbors. To my surprise, I found that this idea walked right into my head as if it were a familiar acquaintance who had the right to enter without knocking, and it hung around, nudging me. This was strange, because making large purchases was by no means customary behavior for me. I had never bought land or a house; I had never bought anything more major than a car. I wondered if perhaps I was going slightly off the deep end, as people who become involved with cults are known to do.

But when I spoke of the land-buying notion to Sylvia, she did not dismiss it as foolish. This was reassuring, because Sylvia's nature was sensible and hard-headed. She was not the sort of person to fly off impetuously into harebrained ventures. As a responsible homeowner, she knew about realistic, no-nonsense things like paying mortgages, replacing hot water heaters, and cleaning out rain gutters. I, on the other hand, while not an irresponsible person, tended to get lost in mental meanderings and do things like leave the flue open so the heat went up the chimney, and forget to unlock the gate for the meterreader, and create rings on the table by putting my wet glass on its surface. "Wandering off," said Sylvia when I did this sort of thing, and she was right. Her attention stuck to the concrete realities much better than mine.

So I was glad to have her as a sounding board for this idea. We talked about it at great length, considered it from many angles, and after all the pros and cons had been sorted through, I thought, Why not? Why *shouldn't* I buy a piece of land in the country? I tried to come up with good reasons not to, but the only one I could think of was that it was the kind of move my father would think was insane: buying forty acres of land next to a Zen Buddhist monastery several miles from a small town in the mountains. "Are you crazy?" he would ask. "Have you lost your mind?"

I felt strangely willing to lose my mind. The craziness of the venture was part of its appeal. When had I ever done anything crazy? I had always done what people expected me to do. Here was a chance to be different.

The Guide said I could buy any forty acres I wanted, except the central portion where the Center's tent was set up. So Sylvia and I became explorers, hacking through the brush, crawling up hillsides dense with manzanita and poison oak, sliding down slopes through dry slippery layers of oak leaves. We walked the boundary of the property, as well as we could, across the ridge of hills on the south, beside the grazing land on the west, and down to the creek at the northwest corner.

From the creek, we scrambled straight up a steep hill, most of the time bent double or crawling on hands and knees to get under the bushes and between them. We separated, so that we'd have two chances of finding the best route, and called to each other to keep track of where we were. "Come this way!" I would shout, and Sylvia would call back, "No, you come this way, there's a clear spot here!" At times I thought we were going in circles. I thought we would never find a place where we could even stand up, and that we'd have to admit defeat and slide back down to the creek. But suddenly, at the top of the hill, we were out in the open. We came to a little clearing, maybe twenty by fifty feet, and in the clearing, as if they had been purposely planted there, were two young trees: a ponderosa and a digger pine.

The slope we stood on descended slightly to the south. If you're going to build something — a small cabin, say, to stay in every now and then — you want it to have a southern exposure so that it's light inside, and you want it to sit up high enough so that you have a view of something, other than just tree trunks. As far as we could tell, this was such a site. Or it would be if it were larger. We thought we were more or less in the middle of the northwest forty acres.

So we decided: I would buy the northwest forty, bounded by the fence along the pasture land to the west and including a stretch of creek and road on the north. The other two sides were in common with Middlefield. We hired a surveyor, who stuck stakes in the ground here and there with neon pink plastic ribbons tied to them, showing where the line of my land lay. We drew up a contract and a schedule of payments. I wrote the biggest check I'd ever written and became a landowner.

Odd, owning land. This land had been here for thousands of years, going about its business of producing trees and grass and harboring wildlife equally well whether anyone owned it or not. It was like those animals in the zoo that you can adopt by paying a certain amount of money for a year. The animals go on as before, living their lives exactly the same way, not knowing that they have been adopted. My ownership of this land was the same sort of thing — a flimsy concept, supported by some pieces of paper and some measurements and some legal agreements.

After a while, I told my family about my purchase. "Are you out of your mind?" said my father. "Who are these Zens, anyway?" he said. "How do you know this outfit isn't going to collapse in a year or two? Then where will you be?"

I gave the most sensible answers I could think of. I talked about contracts and contingency agreements and investment value, but really I had no answer to his underlying question: How do you know that this is a sound venture? I didn't know. Maybe the Center would fold. Maybe I'd try to sell my forty acres and find that no one would buy it, and it would be as though I'd dug a hole in the dirt and buried my money. Maybe Sylvia and I would go live there and discover that we detested country living, with its violent weather and remoteness from movie theaters. I didn't know. I didn't care. I felt as if I had come to the edge of a cliff and taken a small but unretractable step out into the air. I didn't know if the ground was an inch below my feet or a hundred miles. I didn't know if I had a parachute. I could feel the wind swishing by under my feet. Suddenly, in stepping away from the edge of the cliff, I found that life is a huge, limitless, three-dimensional space, possibilities in all directions, and I was, to my astonishment, willing to wait and see whether I'd fall or fly.

5

The Hermitage

The full-time monastic life, Sylvia and I knew, was not for us. But we did plan to spend some substantial periods of time at Middlefield and so we qualified for a hermitage of our own — a little plywood shack like those of the permanent residents. We chose a spot just off the dirt road that ran along the southern border of my forty acres. It was a hollow in which a tree had fallen years ago and was now lying on its side, smooth and silvery, like a low garden wall.

The hermitage got built in stages, whenever a few people were around to work on it. The first stage was the floor — a slightly elevated platform, eight feet wide and sixteen feet long, surfaced with plywood. We spread our sleeping bags on it, finding the platform a great improvement over the ground. After a while the frame of two-by-fours was nailed up and topped with the roof of ripply galvanized tin, creating a kind of gazebo or pavilion, a roofed place open to the air, protecting us from bird poop and falling acorns, but not from weather. Then came the first set of walls: black plastic tacked to the two-by-fours, and translucent plastic over the window holes. We rejoiced in our closed-in structure, which had the playful and enchanting quality of the kind of fort you make as a child by hanging sheets over a card table. But a windstorm one night ripped the plastic off its nails. We replaced it with stiff black tarpaper, which made the house a bit gloomy but comparatively solid and tight. Finally, one week when people and time came available, we cut the plywood into wall-sized pieces and nailed it up. We put in the windows we'd bought at a salvage yard, a matching set with frames painted dark red, nearly the color of manzanita bark, and we hung in the doorway an ancient wooden screen door with scabby white paint and no handle. Our hermitage was complete.

This process was a nice capsule illustration of the principle of the search for better accommodation, which pulls humankind along by the nose. Each stage of the building was adequate at first — more than adequate, luxurious. But that which is luxurious decays, over time, into that which is adequate, and adequate is by definition not really very good. People have too much imagination to be content with adequate. Too many possibilities occur to us. If we could do this, why not that? So we make improvements, and what had seemed luxuries before become, in retrospect, privations. Sylvia and I looked back from the standpoint of our finished hermitage and thought, How did we cope before we had walls? How could we have borne that dark old tarpaper? The truth is, we had a good time at every stage, as long as the new feature remained an improvement over the stage before rather than the primitive predecessor to the stage afterward.

Sylvia dug up two manzanita sprouts and planted them in the front of the building. We decided to call the place Manzanita Cottage, but we never did. We always just called it the hermitage.

The next step was to furnish it. At one end of the room we installed a steamer trunk, a dark green antique with slats of wood bolted to it. This was where we stashed our sleeping bags when we weren't staying at the hermitage. If we left them on the cots, they were likely to have mice and spiders in them by the time we came back. The top of the trunk made a place to sit and a table to set things on, although, because it was slightly domed, whatever we set there tended to topple over. At the other end of the room we put two canvas and aluminum cots, mine against the north wall, Sylvia's against the south, beneath the big double window. We put a slab of foam rubber on each one, and sleeping bags on top, and we had beds that were low to the ground, rather swaybacked, but acceptable.

For seating we had two fold-up aluminum lawn chairs with striped plastic webbing, the low kind of chair that makes your knees jut up higher than your lap and puts your seat about five inches from the ground. For light we had flashlights and a propane lamp. For shelves, we nailed some pieces of two-by-four horizontally between the posts of the house, and on them we put the items that this simple life required: two cups, our toothbrushes and toothpaste, insect repellent, hand lotion, a jar of peanuts, a box of tea bags, and a coffee pot in which to heat water over our Sterno flame.

We pounded nails in the wall to hang our clothes from. We put up a mirror, with a shelf under it for a comb, a brush, and a hand mirror so Sylvia could see the back of her head, where her hair, after she'd been lying on it all night, swirled out in a kind of pinwheel that she called her bald spot, though it was not bald at all. On the same shelf was a plastic cup with fingernail scissors and nail files in it, and tweezers for pulling out the chin hairs that do not stop growing just because you're leading a pure and vigorous life.

When we were finished, we had a small marvel of comfort and convenience, relatively speaking. Still, the hermitage remained a permeable house, a house that let things in. Smells came in, the smell of dry grass, of rain on dirt, sometimes a faint waft of outhouse smell if it was a hot day and the wind was right. The litter of nature came in. Oak leaves wedged between the floor-boards, dead bugs collected in the bottoms of cups and at the backs of shelves. Shreds of dry grass came in on our shoes, burrs came in on our pants. Mice invaded when we weren't there and made nests in the Kleenex box. A lizard crept inside and died among the kindling. Spiders walked down the walls, lacewings crawled up the screens, moths killed themselves in the propane lamp. Once, when we arrived after being away for a while, we noticed some black rice-like droppings on the shelf beneath the mirror. Gingerly, I touched the mirror's frame, and from behind it a bat sprang out, flapped into our faces, and swooped around the room in swift silent scallops while we scrambled for the door.

We took our showers outside. Our shower was a plastic bag we filled with water in the morning, set in the sun during the day, and hung in an oak tree in the evening, its water heated to shower temperature or beyond, depending on the warmth of the day. Sylvia made a shower floor, a rectangle of wood with smooth slats across it, for us to stand on. A branch that poked out perpendicular to the trunk of the tree was our towel rack. I had not known before how lovely it is to take a shower in the woods at the end of a hot day. Just standing naked outside is a rare experience. Where can you do it, unless you're the bold sort of person who goes to nude beaches, or unless you go camping in remote unpeopled country? Even your own back yard is not private enough. Here, I could shed my clothes in the hermitage, walk outside wearing only my rubber flip-flops, and stand under the tree training the spray of hot water all over me, feeling the breeze on all my surfaces. One bagful of water supplied two perfectly adequate hot showers. Sylvia squirted the soap off my back, I squirted it off hers.

At night we brushed our teeth under the trees, spitting toothpaste suds onto the ground. We hung our daytime clothes on nails and put on our night clothes — one thin shirt in summer, many layers of T-shirts, long underwear, socks, and sweatsuits in winter. I stayed up as long as I could, reading, writing in my journal: if you go to bed at nine o'clock, especially in winter, it will not be day for many hours, too many to spend in a bed that makes your back hurt. Sylvia, not having this problem, went to bed early. She valued her eight hours of sleep. If she didn't get them, a mysterious malady called "hot head" would afflict her the next day. She claimed it was like having a head stuffed with hot cotton, and it made thinking difficult. So she blocked out the light, and the noise of my pages turning or my nose snuffling, by burrowing down into her sleeping bag so that only a few sprouts of hair showed. "I'm going under," she would say. "Don't stay up long."

I tried to, but I never could. Sometimes it was too hot, and unbearable to have the propane lamp adding its several degrees just over my shoulder. Sometimes it was too cold, and the freezing air penetrated all my layers. Sometimes it was just too uncomfortable in that low slant-backed foldup chair. So I went to bed, too, completing the routine: Get the yellow bucket (our nighttime chamber pot) from under the house; latch the screen door, just in case a killer is drifting around in the woods; put the flashlight between the beds; blow out the propane lamp. Slide myself carefully into my sleeping bag so as not to tip the cot over sideways, turn off the flashlight, settle back, whisper "Night-night, Syl," very softly in case she is already asleep. Look out through the light black squares of the windows at the stars above the dark profile of the hills and trees. Watch the moon, if there is one, traveling across the sky, making a pale patch on Sylvia's sleeping bag. Doze off.

Often, living this rustic life, we would look at each other and smile goofy smiles. "Isn't this great?" we would say. "So simple, so beautiful." But we didn't go around in a daze of contentment all the time. On plenty of occasions, we did not have fun. The hermitage felt crowded, and we bumped into each other, gritting our teeth, breathing loudly in exasperation. The heat made us itchy and snappish. The cold scared us. Everything was rickety. The table I made out of warped boards rocked. Mosquitoes buzzed in through the hole in the screen door. The propane lamp smoked. Once, when the temperature had been over a hundred for days and we had bug bites and poison oak, and dusty rivers of sweat ran down our legs and sides, Sylvia gave me a dire look and said, "This place sucks, doesn't it?"

And this was true. As well as being a wonderful place, it was a miserable place. But then so is everywhere, at one time or another. The whole world has the same problems: too hot, too cold, full of spiders and bad smells. You can protect yourself from all this, or you can let your protections dissolve a little, you can become slightly more permeable, like the hermitage, and let things in. You feel a little closer to the world, more like a participant than an observer, when you allow yourself to be hot and cold and bug-ridden along with it.

6

Zen Practice:
Saving All Sentient Beings

Many zillion bugs live at Middlefield. In the summer they hum and whine and buzz like an orchestra warming up to play some monotonous, chromatic, endless piece of music. The bugs provide a constant background noise, almost like wind, only it's made up of infinite, tiny, zigzag hairs of sound. The noise makes the air seem thick, causing you to think of the terrific *distribution* of bugs, how there is one in just about every small piece of space, so that no matter where you stand in those three hundred and twenty acres, the warming-up orchestra sounds about the same. If you took all the bugs and magnified their size by ten — say, for instance, if you made a fly the size of a pingpong ball — the bug density might be so great that you couldn't walk around without having to breast-stroke your way through a seething bug soup.

One great fault of bugs is that they do not, like larger animals, run the other way when they see people. More often they flock toward us, hover around us enthusiastically, and aim to settle in.

We have to have a relationship with them, whether we want one or not.

Usually a person's feeling for a bug is a mixture of fear, loathing, and irritation, with the tension of a power struggle added in. We are bigger and smarter than bugs, but they are more numerous, and nastier. They have too many legs, and eyes that you can't look into. Their bodies are like tiny brittle plastic bottles with horrible syrup inside. Because they bite and sting and tickle us, burrow under our skin, hang in clouds in front of our eyes, inject us with diseases, and chew holes in our rose blooms, it's hard not to conclude that they are out to get us. Our response is to want to get them first.

I have had this relationship with bugs both in nightmares and in real life: I try to kill them; they remain stubbornly alive, maimed and writhing; I am thrown into a blind panic of revulsion. Die, die, I hate you! is what the relationship comes down to.

At Middlefield, we try to find a different relationship with bugs. For example: In the late summer occasionally we see tarantulas crossing the dirt roads. A tarantula, with a hairy body the size of a cherry tomato, is an evil-looking spider, though relatively harmless. I imagine that in other places people routinely stomp on tarantulas when they run into them. Here, we watch them protectively as they make their way along. We might put one in a plastic cup and show it around a bit, but we soon set it down again where we found it and stand there like crossing guards while it goes on its way.

All kinds of bugs receive the same solicitous treatment. The Guide will bring hermitage construction to a halt to carry a spider out of range of a hammer; she will pluck a tick off her leg and set it safely on a leaf; she will pick up the most violent-looking insects as tenderly as if they were kittens. I saw her do this once with a huge, fleshy, striped beetle of a sort I'd never seen before. My reaction to it was curiosity. I wanted to study the beetle, turn it over with a stick and look at its belly, nudge it and see how it moved. She wanted only to get it out of the way so no one would step on it. She didn't look around for a piece of paper to put it on but instead let it crawl onto her hand. "Come on, sweetie," she said, and set the bug off the road, under a tree.

So now let's just face the question of whether this is ridiculous or not, because that's what arises in people's minds when they see such great care taken for the lower orders of living things. Critics of this behavior are likely to state that bug rescuing is stupidly sentimental, that it's a waste of time, that it's dangerous, even, because it takes attention away from what is really important. They are likely to toss moral dilemmas at people who rescue bugs: "You can't avoid killing things," they say. "It's built into life. Bugs fly against the windshield of your car. Are you going to give up driving? Are you going to give up eating because bugs die when the fields are plowed? Are you going to let people die of malaria so you don't have to kill mosquitoes?"

You answer these questions with either Yes or No, and you're going to find yourself in trouble. The problem is that the questions are based on a mistaken premise.

The third of Buddhism's Three Pure Precepts is the vow to benefit all sentient beings. Is a bug a sentient being? If it can suffer, we can call it sentient. How do we know if a bug suffers or not? If you pull some of the legs off a spider and watch it drag itself in ragged circles, does it seem to be suffering? If you squish half of a beetle and watch the other half scratching at the air, it *looks* as if it is suffering. We don't know for sure. We can never know for sure what the feeling is in any body besides our own.

When I was a child, I invented, in my mind, a machine that you could attach to two people, a boxlike thing with cables coming out of it, and a little lever on top. When you turned the lever one way, the person on the right would feel the pain of the person on the left, and when you turned the lever the other way, the flow would reverse. This machine, I figured, would solve the problem of other people's underestimation of my pain and consequent indifference to it. If I were to say, "I have an awful stomachache," and the other person said, "Oh, really?" in a bored voice, I could hook us up to the machine, turn on the current, and wait for that person to say, "Yow, that hurts! Poor you! Now I understand!" (I would, of course, be able to experience other people's pains, too, my sister's migraines and eczema, for instance, though this was not foremost in my mind when I invented the machine.)

Without this machine, however, I have no clue about the feelings of other beings except for the feelings that arise in me in response. Maybe a half-mashed insect feels pain, maybe it doesn't. But what I feel when I look at that injured bug is a kind of nausea. I want to turn away. I curl up my mouth and grimace in a way that I wouldn't if, say, I tore the petals off a flower. Whether the bug suffers or not, I find that *I* seem to suffer.

And this, according to the Guide, is the thing to pay attention to. Do you see yourself in that beetle, or squirrel, or dog? Do you find that you wince a little when its leg is broken or you see it squashed on the side of the highway? Maybe you wince if it's a dog but not if it's a squirrel, or maybe if it's a squirrel but not a beetle.

Saving all sentient beings is more like a direction you walk in than a destination you achieve. You could think of it as a road on which you can walk either way. At one end of the road, far off to the east, let's say, there is a destination called, "I feel no more pain than I can help." At the other end, far to the west, is a destination called, "I feel the pain of everything as my own." You can head toward either place, and you can be very far from your destination or very close to it, though probably only a few people ever actually reach either end.

At the very far east end of this road is the person who has succeeded in disregarding the pain of absolutely everything. Even his own pain he is only selectively aware of. He is the one who can do harm of the most atrocious kinds without a twinge of discomfort, because nothing is real to him outside his own skin. It is all separate, all dead matter. To him, the world looks like a billion separate beings, each one grimly intent on living at all costs, each one fighting against the others for the scarce means of survival. If one gains, another has to lose. The one who is most crafty, ruthless, and powerful wins.

At the far west end of the road is the person who feels the pain of everything — from the stressed-out executive, to the deer seen through the rifle sight, to the bug with its delicate leg. This is not someone sitting on the ground howling in agony, bombarded by all that pain to the point of craziness. It is someone who has come to see no difference between her own self and the rest of the world, someone whose skin has in a sense dissolved and fallen away, so that she sees everything as part of her own being. She is not a "good" person, in the sense of virtuous, socially responsible, doing her duty, altruistic. She refrains from harming things as she would refrain from chopping off her own arm.

What does the world look like to such a person? Maybe like this: Say you're looking out at a lake, and you see twenty strange scallop-shaped creatures swimming out there in a row. You shoot a bullet through one of them. Instead of seeing that one disappear and the others remain, the whole twenty sink out of sight. What you've really seen was the back of a sea serpent looping in and out of the water. Down below, the animal composed of all the loops has been killed. The person who is at the far west end of the road realizes that down below life's teeming surface, in the depths that we can't see, all creatures are like limbs of the same great body.

For a long time, we have been training ourselves in separateness. We have considered it practical and necessary to harden up inside, to be the sensible sort of people who choose highways and dams over dwindling species of fish and birds, who feel not a tremor when the car hits a possum, who eat lamb chops and either do not think about the lamb cut apart to make them, or think about it briefly and remind ourselves that life is tough, and you can't get sentimental about animals, or where will it end?

It isn't easy to turn around and start walking in the other direction on that road that can lead either toward or away from suffering, but we can practice for it in whatever small ways present themselves. We can transport spiders out of the path of danger, if we are willing to be thought mildly ridiculous; we can give over part of the vegetable garden to the gophers and the deer; we can stop shutting the lamb and the pig and the cow out of our imaginations, which will make us less and less interested in eating their legs and sides and rumps. We aren't going to achieve complete harmlessness; but we can take some steps in that direction. As the Vietnamese Zen monk Thich Nhat Hanh says, the fact that we steer by the North Star doesn't mean we expect to arrive there.

The point of saving all sentient beings is not to ensure the personal health and happiness of every bug, bird, fish, and animal on the planet. It is simply to foster the attitude that leads away from suffering. We can't change the world so that no one gets sick, no one is hurt, no one dies. The best we can do is take care of suffering where we find it. We save all beings because in the process of doing so we expand the boundaries of our identity; we push out the fences that limit what we can love.

7

House Enchantment

■

I can't remember now if there was a time when we did not plan to build something more permanent than the hermitage on the land I had bought. Maybe there was, but it didn't last long. The urge to build on a plot of empty ground is probably embedded in our genes.

We would build a cabin, we decided — a one-room cabin, very simple, a sort of rustic studio apartment. It would give us a bit more space and comfort than the hermitage.

At home in the evenings, we began to talk about this cabin. Our best talks were during cocktail hour, the time after work and before dinner when we settled down in the living room and told each other how our days had gone. I sat on the couch with my Scotch and water, Sylvia sat on the striped chair with her beer, and we described to each other the ways a one-room house could be, how the kitchen should be at the east end so it would get the morning sun, and the fireplace should be at the west end so you could see the sunset out the window beside it.

On days when we didn't have to work, we went to breakfast at the restaurant down the street, where they had pink paper placemats on the white tablecloths and small vases with real flowers in them. Vivaldi played on the sound system, sprightly but unobtrusive. We drank spiced tea and ate eggs with fried potatoes and scones, and as we ate, we talked about our house and drew floor plans on the pink placemats.

We were aiming for simplicity. Our lives in town had filled up with clutter. Some of it was tangible clutter — piles of magazines waiting to be read, old double-boilers and Chinese bamboo steamers sitting unused at the back of kitchen cupboards, boxes of flowered notepaper, sweaters we might or might not wear again. Some of it was intangible clutter that blew around in the air like litter in a strong wind: dentist appointments, car repairs, phone calls from survey takers and newspaper subscription departments, helicopter traffic reports on car radios. Our house in the country would eliminate clutter simply by having no room for it.

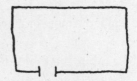

The more we talked, the more pictures we drew, the more we became enchanted by the vision of our house. We thought about it all the time. What happens when you give something that much ardent attention is that it starts to grow. It blossoms in the warmth of your love. This is what the house did. It bulged out a few feet here and there, acquired some conveniences, and began to shimmer with possibilities.

Before long it was growing wildly and pulling us along behind. It sat in its clearing undergoing one transformation after another,

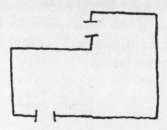

and with each one the life we imagined there took on a more alluring reality. Peace and beauty, said the house; mornings you chop wood as the sun rises; evenings you sit on the veranda and watch the sunset. Deer stroll past the door; the sound of the monastery bell floats up from below. It will be, promised the house, a life that calms the nerves and nourishes the spirit.

We had talked, over the years, in a wistful, unrealistic way, about living in the country. Every time we went on a trip, we'd look around and say, What would it be like to live here? We'd point to charming dilapidated houses and guess that we could probably buy them for almost nothing. We'd talk, depending on where we were, about having an old stone manor in an apple orchard, or an adobe built around a courtyard in the desert, or a Victorian cottage on a cliff overlooking the ocean. We knew these were fantasies. We forgot about all those places as soon as we got home.

But this was different. This place had stretched out a strong hand and grabbed us by the shirtfronts. At some point, almost without our noticing, we had decided to make the drastic change: simplify our lives, clarify our purposes, and move to the country.

So the house got more complicated. Walls divided the interior. We'd need room in the kitchen to store food, because the market would no longer be down the street; commodious closets, to hold our bulky winter clothes; a wide porch where we could sit in the shade on summer days; rooms with doors, in which we could be alone. Light should come in from at least two sides of every room, we agreed; but to make this happen you had to have a house that turned corners. We drew and redrew, figuring out ways to have everything.

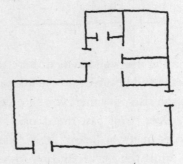

Somehow, unless we both fell heir to large fortunes within the next year or so, we would need paying work to live there full-time. I thought vaguely of writing for computer companies and sending my work down out of the mountains over the phone wires; Sylvia thought vaguely of working for the Center, doing bookkeeping and office management. To do these things you need an office, and so we added one. The house became a lopsided U-shape.

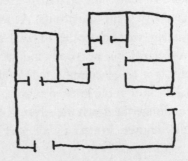

And finally it grew right off the paper into the third dimension: We added a tower room, for meditation and for looking out at the view.

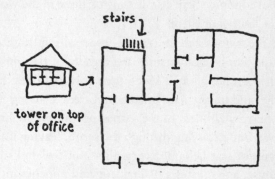

By then we were slaves to house enchantment. Out the window of the car, in walks around the neighborhood, in whatever magazines and books fell into our hands, we looked at houses and judged their beauty. In meetings at work, I drew floor plans, rooflines, and elevations on my memo paper. I made a cardboard model, complete with little doors that opened and a roof that came off to show the rooms inside. I was in love with the new house, and with the life we would live there.

That was in the daytime. At night, black glasses came down over my eyes. Everything changed. I remembered that being close to nature means being far from restaurants and supermarkets. It means driving long distances to get a bottle of olive oil. I was used to having everything I needed within five minutes of my house. What if the store up there had the wrong kind of granola? What if the produce was wilted, and the only lettuce iceberg?

And then there was the loneliness of life in the country. People don't drop by when you live up a dirt road that's off another dirt road, off a gravel road that's five miles from town. The monks are silent; Sylvia and I would have only each other to talk to; we would grow listless and simple-minded from lack of stimulation. And what if we couldn't get work up there and had to take jobs as part-time waitresses at the Pine Tree Cafe? What if the Center moved somewhere else, leaving us alone in the woods with no reason for being there?

And the woods can be terrible, especially at night. Nature is all around, not beautiful nature, but dreadful nature. Just beyond your thin walls are animals living their tortured lives: hunching against the cold on the bare branches of trees, clawing their way through narrow lightless tunnels, rooting and scrambling in the dead leaves, and prowling through the scrub, leaving little lumps and pebbles of scat behind. Every night, an owl sinks its talons into a mouse, a fox seizes a flailing frog and punches into its soft ballooning belly. Nature is appalling. At night it made good sense to me that people should band together in cities and put a lot of concrete between themselves and such nightmares. At night I knew that this plan of ours was a mistake.

In the daytime the excitement took over again, hope revived, and I drew more pictures.

The trouble was, I was two different people. The day person brushed aside the concerns of the night person. The night person was dumbfounded by the foolishness of the day person. Sylvia had the same two people in her. We talked about it. Should we go forward or not go forward? We discussed this in the evenings, after dinner, when we could feel the night persons coming on. We sat down with paper and pencil and totted up the pros and cons. Often, on paper, the cons won. We looked at each other and said, "Shall we back out? Shall we forget the whole thing?" When you have two opposites clamoring at each other like that, each one throwing out facts and feelings and opinions in a loud contentious voice, how do you tell which voice is *real*? We understood, finally, that it was not to be figured out that way. Both voices were real. Neither one was any more real than the other. Outside of the pros and cons, on a completely different level, the house enterprise was moving forward, and we were moving with it. That's just how it was. The pros and cons were irrelevant. Which is better, night or day? You can't have one without the other. The turning of the world is what you finally have to go with.

8

Zen Practice:
All Things Are Without a Self

I sit on my round black cushion, hands in my lap, legs crossed, eyes cast down at the correct angle. I tingle all over with serious intention. What do I really want? Really, fundamentally, most of all in my life? Today I am sure: What I really want is peace, interior silence, a glimpse of the oneness of all things. What I really want is to transcend the mind, which gets in the way of realization. I do want this. I do, desperately. Whatever measure of enlightenment I can achieve in this lifetime, that's what I want more than anything.

The meditation begins. *Bong*, the big bell. *Ting*, the small bell. I sit. My attention follows my breathing, like a bloodhound following a scent, like a searchlight following a plane. This time I will stay right with it; it won't get away from me. Up and down. In and out. This breath, the next breath. They are slightly shallow breaths, there's a constriction in my chest. I seem to be tense. Why am I tense?

That is the chink into which the thought wedges its toe. I am tense, my breathing is shallow. Rubber bands are wrapped around my chest. Why? Every traumatic event, I recall reading somewhere, is translated from the emotional into the physical and becomes a spot of tension, a pain, a habitual tic or way of moving. All my disappointments and terrors have left their marks on me, and this tightness in the breathing is certainly one of them. It is not an ordinary tightness. I have been noticing it lately; the tightness occurs in certain situations and accompanies certain patterns of thought. If I could see the connections clearly, I could get to the bottom of it. I am on to something here. I need to think about this.

(But you wanted not to think. You were going to transcend the mind.)

In a minute, I will. This is important.

Time passes. One thought leads to another. I consider childhood fears, the origin of conditioning, the proper education of children, the education of my niece, my niece's approaching birthday, the virtues of chocolate cake with raspberry filling between the layers. Now and then I surface briefly, berate myself, attend ferociously to my breath for a while, and sink out of sight again. *Ting*, the small bell. *Bong*, the big bell. I look back at my wasted half hour. I sigh in disgust. I am no good. My will is rotten. I fool myself when I say I want enlightenment. Discouragement settles on me like a fog. I can't do this, I have no resolution. I am not a strong steel rod of passionate purpose but a pile of litter blowing around in the wind. Any cheap trick can capture me. I am ordinary and petty and self-involved, right down to the core.

I have in my mind a picture of my self, this self that I am so unhappy with: it is a solid thing, something like a statue. A statue has certain fixed qualities that can be enumerated. You can look at a statue and say, It is white, unpainted, made of marble, depicts a woman with hair pulled back and a serene expression.

I imagine that my self is similar: it is a thing with qualities, and I can look at it, if I am perceptive enough, and say, I am . . . and then list the ten or fifty qualities that characterize my self. It would be best if these were all positive qualities. This is the correct sort of self to have, one that is, say, courageous, loving, honest, intelligent, clear, and strong. *My* self, however, is not what it should be. Sometimes it exhibits some of those qualities, other times their opposites. Right now, for instance, it is weak when it should be strong, and muddy when it should be clear. It is as if the statue has a splotch of bird poop on it, or a chunk gouged out of the forehead. There is something wrong with it; it's not as it should be. The obvious solution is to fix it. Make it stronger! Clean the spots off! Whip it into shape! I have been hammering away at this repair job for forty-some years; my efforts should be having an effect by now. And yet the defects of my self are just as glaring as they ever were.

I can draw one of two conclusions from this failure: either I am a hopeless weakling, too puny or too lazy to hammer hard enough; or I am mistaken about the nature of the problem and the tool to use on it — I am trying, perhaps, to put in a screw with a hammer, to cure a stomachache with a socket wrench. Either of these conclusions might be true, but there is more promise in considering an alternate view of the problem than in deciding that I am a hopeless weakling. What might that other view be?

Buddhism has a suggestion: All things are *without* a self, it says. This is hard to grasp. My self seems so extremely present, so almost tangible, so like a *thing* — except in its habit of displaying completely opposite qualities at different times. A statue doesn't do this. I don't look at the statue one day and see that it's made of marble, look at it the next day and see that it's made of sandstone, and then try to puzzle out which is the *real* statue, the marble or the sandstone. But this is what I do with my self: which is the *real* me, weak and murky, or strong and clear?

Perhaps my self does not exist in exactly the same way as the statue. It changes all the time. I can't say what its qualities are in any permanent way, only what they are at a given moment. It is less like an object than like a space occupied by a jostling crowd — like a railroad station with crowds surging this way and that, shouting and gabbling and contending with each other, or like a stage with an extremely complicated and incomprehensible play going on, where one actor after another elbows his way to the front and declaims his piece, or like a terrible family party, rife with tensions and hidden animosities and flareups and secret alliances. An ever-changing drama is going on in me; I am just the space that holds it.

Who are these people that live in my head, then? When I start to look at myself this way, I begin to see: some of them are old children — a thousand versions of myself at other ages, myself frozen in a protective reaction to the world. Some are other people. I have built a replica of my mother inside me for permanent reference. It says what she would say, advising me on matters of taste and behavior. I've got my father in there, too, keeping an eye on my finances, reminding me that I tend to be lazy and careless. Each of these beings is set on perpetuating its own existence. Each has a purpose it is striving to fulfill, an urgent message to convey. "Be careful!" is the watchword of one of them. "You must find love or you will die," is the refrain of another. Often they come in pairs: "Everything you say is stupid and embarrassing," one says, and its partner, on other occasions, says "You are far smarter than most of those nincompoops out in the world." They come when the situation calls them into action. Each one, in its turn, takes as much of the space as it can grab; it persuades me, while it's front and center, that it is my self.

I collected these beings to begin with because they were useful defenses against the dangerous world. But now they're acting autonomously. They've formed a society that operates noisily inside me, with all the clashes and inefficiencies of a society, all the loud propaganda, strict though senseless and out-of-date laws, crime in the streets, and dead-end pursuits that societies are subject to. And they offer me the same illusory sense of order that a society provides: I have the feeling, if I don't look too hard, that I know what's going on. I know who I am, I know what's right and wrong, I know what I'm supposed to do. The truth is that this society has gathered momentum over the years and found its own purposes; it lost, long ago, any sense of obligation to the organism as a whole.

What I've been trying to do is turn this chaotic society into a smoothly functioning city, a little internal utopia: ferret out the bad elements, throw them in jail or execute them, pin stars on the heroes and saints and put them on the city council. But the criminals and derelicts and frauds and melancholics keep popping back up, as they do in any society. I can't get rid of them.

And here is the terribly difficult, terribly *counter-intuitive* secret: I must do what seems like exactly the wrong thing. My instinct is to try harder and harder to fix what's wrong, go at it from every conceivable angle, strain until my face turns purple. But my only salvation is to turn away and walk in the other direction.

The internal society thrives on attention. The more I struggle with it, the stronger it gets. If it can be thought to have a collective will, that will is aimed at persuading me that every problem it presents must be solved. I must *figure it out*. But the more I try to figure it out, the more confused I get by the clamor of voices. It's better by far simply to leave town. The voices will only scream more loudly, of course, to reach me; they will throw out not only desperately urgent problems, but enticing landscapes to explore, germs of ideas that will save the world, ancient griefs that must be felt again, injustices that must be righted, catastrophes that will certainly occur unless I rouse myself and avert them. All I have to remember is to *form no relationship* with any of this — neither fight it nor fall for it.

But I can't remember.

Except for now and then, almost by accident. My inner vision readjusts, the way my eyes refocus when I look from the page of the book in front of me to the tree outside the window. This is not the same fending off and stamping down that I ordinarily do. It is an altogether different movement, and it seems to happen on a different level from the clamor of the voices. It's like the feeling I have when I've been dreaming one of those dreams in which I'm being thwarted at every turn — I have forgotten to feed my cat, she is at home starving, but my car won't start, and I have no dime for the phone, and when I find one the phone line is dead, and a man with a knife is coming around the corner — and then I solve the predicament by waking up. The problem unravels. I rise above it. I see with a calm detachment that I do not have to solve it at all.

Who, then, is the "I" that rises above?

I ask the Guide this. "Yes," she says. "Who?"

9

The Nose of the Snake

■

Once we decided to build a house, a chain of events began. It was the kind of chain where you must take a blind step before you can see the next link. Then suddenly there it is, and you realize that it's connected to the link before. And it's connected in a surprising, unexpected way, to something you could never have figured out for yourself. You get a sense, after a while, that there is up ahead another link, and that if you can be tuned in enough, listen hard enough in some way that doesn't have to do with your ears, you will find it.

Of course the chain of events goes all through your life, but there are times when you feel the strength of it in a way that you don't when you're just idling along, or when you're caught in a stagnant pool that seems to have no outlet. These times when the current accelerates have the feel of intention behind them. Now we're into it! Now we're going in the right direction! We must be, look how things are falling into place.

The chain seemed to begin in Bell's Bookstore, though I know it began a long time before that. I went to the bookstore to look for pictures of houses. If Sylvia and I were going to build a house on my forty acres, we needed some ideas about all the different ways houses could look. You don't just say, Build a house, and a house appears. You have to figure out first what sort of house it will be.

I was in charge of research, because aesthetics were my specialty. Sylvia's specialty was the practical. Not that she didn't have aesthetic preferences, which were in fact very much like mine; but she got less riled up about them than I did. It was conceivable to her that a compromise might at some point be necessary between beauty and budget, and she could accept that prospect with equanimity, as I could not. How you decide who takes charge of what is to ask yourself this question: Who will be the most upset if it doesn't get done to her standards? That person gets the job.

I had looked at pictures in the library, but all the houses I saw were wrong. They were either too elaborate, like the ones in *Architectural Digest*, which had curling stairways and art objects on built-in pedestals and Oriental rugs and handcrafted paneling, or they were too funky, like the houses built of scraps of wood in the sixties and seventies, those oddly shaped houses with lots of handmade glass and macramé hangings. We wanted something simple and somehow organic, something that looked as if it belonged there, something that had a quality of simplicity and beauty and utility all at once.

So I stood in front of the ceiling-high bookshelf at Bell's and stared at the titles of books about architecture. A woman who worked there came up behind me. "Can I help you find something?" she said. Usually in bookstores I say no, because I want to look at everything and don't want to know beforehand what I'm going to find, but this time I was already frustrated; the only pictures of houses I had seen so far were unsatisfactory. Too modern, with flat roofs and picture windows; too showy;

too much like the sort of house a family of five would have in a suburb, or in the sort of countryside where they had a horse paddock out back, and a pool. All wrong. So I said maybe she could help me and explained my problem.

"Do you know Christopher Alexander?" she asked. She reached for a fat, pale yellow book with a cover that had no pictures on it. It looked like a boring, scholarly sort of book, but it had a promising title: *The Timeless Way of Building*. A rather grand, poetic-sounding title, but it was the direction in which I was thinking: timeless, not some style that had the indelible stamp of the eighties on it, not someone's idea of The House of the Eighties, but a house that would be beautiful a hundred years from now, and would have been beautiful a hundred years ago.

I opened the book. It had black and white pictures, not very many of them, and they were all of buildings from other times and other places. White thick-walled houses on the islands of Greece; the edge of a steep farm roof somewhere in Scandinavia; a monastery cascading down the side of a hill in Asia; a room with great tall windows on three sides of it, sun pouring in. I scanned the text. The vision I'd been seeking shone in every sentence my eye fell on.

"There is one timeless way of building. It is thousands of years old, and the same today as it has always been."

"Each one of us has, somewhere in his heart, the dream to make a living world, a universe."

"The fact is that the difference between a good building and a bad building, between a good town and a bad town, is an objective matter. It is the difference between health and sickness, wholeness and dividedness, self-maintenance and self-destruction."

"To make a building egoless, the builder must let go of all his willful images, and start with a void."

Some buildings, Christopher Alexander said, were alive and some were not. He spoke of a "pattern language," which arises from within a culture that has deep roots and in which people "live close to their own hearts." He wrote, "In a life which is truly lived, there are no moments which are 'in between' or 'out of life' — every moment is lived fully. The Zen master says, 'When I eat, I eat; when I drink, I drink; when I walk, I walk.' A building or a town which is alive has the same quality."

A house that's alive! It was the very thing we wanted. I bought the book, though it cost forty dollars. I'm not sure I've bought more than three or four books in my life that cost forty dollars, but I knew I must buy this one.

That was the first link, then: the woman in the bookstore who handed me the book. I read it avidly; I began to talk all the time about Christopher Alexander. I went on about him so much that people laughed when I brought up his name. But no one I talked to had ever heard of him, until I mentioned him to Jerome, the art director at work. Oh, sure! said Jerome, he'd read the book, and not only that, he had the second one in the series, *A Pattern Language*. I borrowed it from him.

Between the pages was a bookmark from the store where Jerome had bought the book. This was the second link in the chain. We went to the store: it was a bookstore all about building, full of every kind of book on building. We looked around, rather dazed, not knowing what we were looking for, overwhelmed and intimidated by books about carpentry and plumbing and electricity, about being your own contractor, about building brick houses and gazebos and stone walls and furniture. Where were the simple books about how to build a house like the ones Christopher Alexander was talking about? Where were the answers to the low-level questions we were puzzling over?

For example: What do you make the house *out of*? As far as I knew, you start with a frame of two-by-fours and then put something on the outside of it. If you are rich, you put wood, real wood, like redwood, or you put stones or perhaps brick. If you are not rich, you put siding. You buy it in sheets at the lumberyard and nail it up. I guess it is actually wood, at least part of it is, but it has a phony look. It looks thin. The sheets are divided by grooves, but everyone knows the grooves don't divide real planks, they are simply meant to look as if they do. I didn't want anything in this house to be trying to look like something it wasn't. An honest house, was what I had in mind, but an honest house that did not require a giant budget.

I'm surprised I even noticed the little spiral-bound book that gave me the answer. It was not really a book, just pages bound with one of those plastic hoops. *The Rammed Earth Experience*, it was called, by David Easton. The first thing I noticed about David Easton was that he lived in a town in the mountains, about an hour's drive from Middlefield. The second thing I noticed was that rammed earth houses, the ones in the photographs in the book, were unlike any pictures of modern houses I'd seen before. They were simple, and they were beautiful.

A rammed earth house is made out of the earth it stands on. You dig the foundation, and the dirt you scoop out becomes the walls. It's mixed with a little concrete, a little sand, and some water, and then packed down into wall-shaped plywood forms until it becomes as hard as stone. Take the forms off, and what you have is a foot-thick wall, smooth and brown, like adobe, only solid, not divided into bricks.

We knew right away that this was what we wanted. It was another piece of magic: that book, standing on the shelf in a bookstore I would never have heard of if I hadn't borrowed *A Pattern Language* from Jerome, which I would never have done if the woman at Bell's hadn't taken Christopher Alexander off the shelf and handed it to me.

It was a lesson in how things happen by themselves. I have always thought I had to make things happen. "Take some initiative!" said my father. I didn't want to, but I thought I should. As I understood it, you had to make yourself do something you otherwise would not do if anything was ever going to happen in your life. You could not sit still, because then you would be left behind, then somehow your life would stop, everything would stagnate, and you would begin to rot. I thought I had to join something, like after-school sports, or the pep club, or the school newspaper. Everyone told me I should join something because it was good for me. No one said, *Pay close attention to whatever it is you love the best, and then the next step will be clear*.

When I was a child I prided myself on my agility. One of the things I could do was jump from one rock to another in places where there was no flat ground in between. Crossing a stream or scrambling along the rocks at the beach by the edge of the waves, I could leap from one rock to the next, placing my sneaker each time in the right place at the last moment. It happened by itself. I didn't have to think — in fact, thinking would have got in the way. There was no time to think. I had to trust my feet to land right, not to slip down the side of the rock, not to twist, not to miss the rock and pitch me over sideways. It was a feeling of suspension, of being right on the edge of the place where this moment becomes the next moment.

I have had a dream, many times, that goes like this: It's dark and I'm running. Usually I'm on a street, or on a path with trees lining it, but I can't see where I'm going, can't see the ground that my foot will land on. Even so, I keep running, with the feel of the darkness breaking like water against my chest. I am willing to abandon myself to it, to put my foot into the darkness and take whatever it presents.

It's the same feeling, the rock-jumping and the running in the dark — as though time is a line moving forward, and has a nose, like the nose of a snake, and behind the nose is the known part, the part we've seen, and in front of it is the unknown. When you ride the nose of the snake, you don't know what is next, not even in the next second. Of course we are always riding the nose of the snake, but we forget it. We trick ourselves into believing that we *do* know what's going to happen next, and we arrange the world, or the world arranges itself, so that this is true a deceptively large amount of the time.

In those days of planning the house, Sylvia and I felt as if we were always riding the nose of the snake. This was a slower ride than leaping from rock to rock or running through the dark in my dream. Still, from day to day, and week to week, we felt ourselves traveling forward into unknown territory, knowing that at any moment the landscape could change abruptly, and willing to make sharp turns or leap at the last moment.

10

Plans on Paper

We took the next large step and hired an architect, a young man just starting out, recommended to us by my sister's husband. Michael, his name was — an earnest, friendly person with lanky brown hair and bushy eyebrows, and between his eyebrows a single long hair that grew all by itself right at the top of his nose. We often asked each other, Sylvia and I, after we'd spent time with him, why he didn't pull that hair out. Didn't it impinge on his line of sight whenever he looked up at a certain angle? Either he was someone who paid remarkably little attention to his appearance, who perhaps never looked at himself in the mirror, or else that hair was for some reason important to him — a charm, maybe, a sign that he'd been touched by a god in a way that gave him an odd bit of magical power. As it turned out, an odd bit of magic did come by way of Michael, though its cause was more likely simple ingenuity than anything supernatural.

We met with him on our living room floor, ate pizza, and talked in detail about the house of our vision. He came back a week or so later with sketches. They showed houses with sharp angles and clean lines: a tall narrow house with a shed roof like a mortarboard, a house whose roof was shaped like a W, a house with a large hole in its facade. All these drawings looked to us modern and effortful, making statements like, "This is a forward-looking house; this is an imaginative house; this house was designed by someone with flair." That was not what we wanted. We wanted our house to say, "This house grew out of the earth. This house has stood here since the beginning of beginningless time, and will stand here long after we're gone. This house is in harmony with the grass and the trees and the sun." So we nixed the first round of drawings and went on to the second.

Many rounds of drawings followed, and much discussion, much balancing of the practical against the visionary. We met at the restaurant down the street and drew on the pink placemats. We met at a coffee house in the city that had small round marble tables and other hard surfaces off which loud jazz rebounded. We met at Michael's office, a cold, gritty place that had formerly been a metal shop, where trains thundered along an elevated track outside the back window and made the whole building rattle. In all these places, we pored over sketches, increasingly excited; the delicate pencil lines, the professional cross-hatchings, the small neat marks that indicated doors and windows — they proved that the house was going to be real.

The building of a house requires hundreds of decisions. We talked endlessly, with Michael and without him, about cabinet space, window sizes, door placement, angles of sunlight, heating systems, roofs.

On the question of the roof, we ran into complications.

What a roof must not have, Michael told us, was "valleys" — places where two sections of roof sloping toward the interior of the house meet in such a way as to lead the rain that falls on them down into a pool with no outlet. The current design of the house made it hard to come up with a roof that didn't have these valleys. He showed us the pictures he had drawn. Not only did the roofs in the pictures have valleys, they were funny looking.

I had seen enough funny looking roofs to know that they completely ruin the appearance of the building beneath them. The Alpine Cottage Apartments, a few miles from our house, for instance, had roofs of such extreme "alpineness," so big, so steep, and so pointy, that the little blue houses underneath looked squashed and cowering. The "modern" houses of the fifties had shed roofs, which I didn't care for either. A shed roof is like a lid set at a slant on a box. It seemed to me a cold, uncaring, unsheltering kind of roof. From the front, the high side, the house is tall and no roof shows. From the back, the low side, the house is squatty and the roof shows too much. You have the feeling that the house has turned its back on you.

We wanted a comforting roof, a beautiful roof, a roof that looked all of a piece with the house. We walked around the neighborhood examining rooflines. People who happened to be at home in the houses we studied must have been puzzled to see us pointing upward, squinting, scuttling around the edges of their lot so as to see the house from all angles. Were we planning a burglary? But we didn't look like burglars, two women more or less well-groomed and openly scanning the premises. Maybe they thought we were admiring the chimney, or that we were bird watchers scoping out a tufted titmouse that had landed on the TV aerial, when actually what we were doing was trying to imprint their roofline on our minds. "It should be like that!" we were exclaiming to each other. "Just like that, except ours would be this way instead of that way, and a little higher here, but see how those two parts go together?" And I would snatch old phone bills out of my purse and make drawings of how it worked so that we could show Michael that it was indeed possible.

There were roof problems other than valleys, too. When you put a roof on a building, you have to consider the length of the space over which the roof has to stretch. The main part of our house would be a long rectangle. Could one roof cover the whole thing? Michael expressed doubt. It would require posts somewhere in the room for support. There would have to be trusses, which are triangular constructions of beams that give the roof strength. When you looked up at the living room ceiling, you would see, in addition to the rafters slanting up to a peak at the center, the cross pieces of the trusses stretching every so often across the width of the room.

All this runs into money, he told us. The house of our imagination was not the same as the house of our budget. Forced to concede the truth of this, we lopped off the tower. It was not a devastating loss — we'd be meditating down the hill in the meditation hall anyway, and if we wanted to look at the distant view, we could set up a ladder and climb to the top of it. But it was the first indication that we were on the downward slope of the design process, the slope where you begin to subtract things instead of adding them.

"If you were to get rid of this office room," Michael said, "the roof would be easier."

We didn't want to get rid of the office. The office was to be not only our room but the Center's too — we would share it. It would have a phone, a computer, and a file cabinet, none of which the Center had. And it was also the symbol of our belief that we could support ourselves up there in the woods. If you have an office, you do office-type work in it, and if you work, then you're likely to be earning some income. If we scratched the office, we'd have to have the computer on the dining room table and papers spread out all over the living room; people from the Center would be sitting in our kitchen, talking on our phone. Somehow, the solution to the roof problem had to include the office.

One day Michael brought us a series of drawings all dealing with the roof problem in different ways. We leafed through them. None pleased us until we saw the last one. In this drawing, the office was split off from the house. It had become a separate building, a little rectangle that stood alone in the crook of the house's two arms.

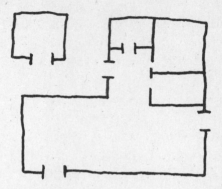

Suddenly the roof was simple. And there was an extra benefit: This plan made a nice separation between home space and office space, so that you could compose your mind differently in the two places, and yet the commute between home and office would be only eight steps across a terrace. Yes, we said, this is the one.

And with that decided, we stamped our approval on the design, and Michael proceeded to do the final drawings. The imaginary house trembled on the edge of reality. Lines on paper and small taped-together pieces of cardboard were ready to become concrete foundations, wooden beams, rammed earth walls. The next steps were the tangible, completely practical ones: get the plans through the building department, put in the septic tank, line up the builders, make a schedule.

The odd piece of magic, the one that may or may not have come about because Michael had some wizardly powers, was this: if it hadn't been for that good idea about the office, nothing would be in this clearing now but the blue pressure tank, sitting lonely and unused on top of the well, a few piles of dead brush, and the birds and deer and rabbits passing through on their way to somewhere else.

11

Fighting the Sticks

Most of the land at Middlefield is covered with dense, spiky woods. You can't walk more than a few steps in any direction without running up against a network of dry twiggy growth — the dead lower branches of the scrub oaks stick out from the trunks in a jagged criss-cross and intersect with the hard red branches of the manzanita, pine needles hung with cobwebs, and long tendrils of poison oak. Try to get through, and leaves slap against your face; they stick to your clothes and travel with you, dropping off onto the outhouse floor, the kitchen tables, the carpet in the meditation hall. You can't stay tidily separate from nature here, there's too much of it. It reaches for you, it clings to you. If you try to push it, it pushes back.

Except for the opening with the two pine trees, nearly all the forty acres was like this. It would be necessary to carve out a space in the tangle of woods if we were going to build a house. We hired a man with a bulldozer to clear the land, and, on a day when we weren't there, he came and scraped the trees off the ground.

We arrived some days later eager to look at our new clearing. I had expected a sense of spaciousness. I had thought that a person standing in the middle of the clearing would be able to see out to the hills, and across to the ridge. Instead, what we had was a strange kind of boxed-in effect. At the top of the hill stood the two pine trees, now looking out over a rectangle of churned-up dirt. On three sides, the sheared-off edge of the woods made a stark line, and at the west end rose a massive wall of crushed trees. All the trees shoved over by the bulldozer were compacted there, bunched and mashed and tangled together, a wreckage of trees stretching out for yards and rising several feet above our heads. It was a miserable sight, like the aftermath of an atrocity, bodies heaped up without dignity. We felt guilty about it, Sylvia especially — she loved the land in its wild state and was deeply reluctant to impose a more human shape on it than was absolutely necessary. "We'll plant more trees," she said, "to make up for this." I agreed. But first the carnage had to be cleared.

We bought ourselves a chainsaw. It came in a bright orange case and had a fourteen-inch blade. We read the manual carefully, more carefully than we read most manuals, because ordinarily the tools we buy are not going to kill us or maim us in hideous ways if we use them wrong. The manual told how to concoct the right mix of chain oil and gasoline, and how to pour it into the correct hole, and how to tell if the chain was too loose or not loose enough. If the chain is too loose, the manual said, it may fly off.

At night I had gruesome chainsaw visions, in which the blade slipped and I sawed off Sylvia's hand, or the chain, which had not been tightened properly, came loose, flew in a berserk loop through the air and wrapped itself around my neck. When we were actually using the chainsaw, the hard substance of reality replaced these visions — we were too occupied with oil cans and funnels, earplugs and goggles, noise, vibrations, flying wood chips, and cracked-open tree trunks to picture anything but what was right in front of our eyes.

It made me feel masterful to use the chainsaw. Usually Sylvia was the best at these rugged kinds of tasks. She was the one who knew how to change an oil filter and drive a truck with a stick shift — skills I had never acquired. But she sprained her wrist on the first day of chainsawing, so most of the actual cutting fell to me. After a while I began to feel competent. This is how you do it: you lay the saw on its side on the ground, making sure the blade is not in gear, and you grab hold of the cord and give it a powerful wrench. The engine chugs a couple of times and opens up into a great blasting furious roar, as if you had seized hold of a sleeping grizzly and it had wakened in a fury. "Okay!" you shout over the noise, and you pick the thing up, bracing your left arm against your hipbone, using your right arm to steer. You lower the blade onto the trunk of a tree and pull the trigger. There's a long scream, sawdust spurts upward, and the wood parts like cake, showing you its clean, innocent, light brown interior. Then it falls away into pieces on either side of the blade.

We developed a method. After choosing a section of the wall to work on, we first focused on getting rid of the leaves and small branches so we could see how the trunks were woven together. We had to study the situation carefully before we chose which trunk to cut, because the trees and branches were so tightly twined around each other that many of them were under pressure. If you cut a branch that was holding down another branch, the one underneath could spring out at you with terrific force. Which branch was safe to cut? It reminded me of those intelligence tests where you have to figure out which lever will turn which wheel and whether the wheel will go to the right or to the left. Sometimes we figured it out wrong, and a tree limb would whip out at us like an angry arm, whacking the saw sideways or cracking us across the legs.

Slowly, we freed one tree after another, dragging them out into the open. As the days went by, the clearing filled up with trunks and branches. In the winter, we said, we would cut the trunks into firewood, and with the leaves and branches we'd make a bonfire, which we would tend while drinking hot chocolate, made in the kitchen of our new house. This vision kept us going through one scorching day after another.

It was a long haul. Every morning, the pile faced us defiantly, barely diminished. We got tired, not just in our muscles, but in our psyches, assaulted by noise, baked by the sun, persecuted by the specklike bugs that hovered before our eyes. A certain grimness crept into our attitude, and a certain tendency to flashes of rage when we hit a stubborn patch. The sense of being masterful waned. We ceased to be conquerors and became more like wrestlers in the last round of some contest that we had not thought would be quite such a challenge, grunting and sweating, determined to struggle through to the end, though realizing now that we'd be banged up in the process. And when at last we had demolished the wall, the boxed-in feeling was only somewhat alleviated. Thick woods still surrounded our clearing. We had forced the trees back, but they looked to me as if they were glowering at us, ready to advance again when they saw their chance.

"We've got to cut some more," I said. "Take out this tree here, and that one, and those manzanitas, and make it all more spacious."

"No," said Sylvia. "We've cut enough. Leave it alone. You're getting obsessed."

I disagreed. I had a vision, not an obsession. A day or so later, hot and sore and irritable, I went out into the woods with the clippers to hack out a few paths for light to come through. The dead branches that stuck out from the trunks were so rotten there was no need to cut them — I just whacked at them with the heavy clippers, and they broke off and fell in pieces, raining dusty powder and catching in my hair. Instead of lying still on the ground, though, they bounced on their springy twigs like big spiders. When I kicked them out of the way, they grabbed my socks and swung along with my foot. The more they misbehaved, the angrier I became, until finally I cast down my clippers in disgust and gave up. The trees had turned against me. They had mean, stubborn, rebellious personalities. I hated them, and it was clear that they hated me, too.

I know that trees don't always feel this way about people. Phyllis told me a story once that confirmed it. She said that during her first year at Middlefield, a year that was very hard for her, the trees by her hermitage scratched her and grabbed at her as nastily as mine did. But after that, they began to change. Now they touch her in a different way. As she goes by, they stretch their branches out and stroke her gently, like blind people identifying a friend with a few light touches, or like unobtrusively helpful park rangers guiding her along the path. The trees have come around, finally; they have become her friends.

It seems that inanimate things are always taking up attitudes: tools that one day bend themselves happily to my purposes the next day turn surly; pieces of furniture are by turns accommodating and annoyingly in the way; trees are gentle or spiteful. It *seems* this way, it's powerfully tempting to see it this way, but I no longer can. Having practiced meditation for some years now, and learned to observe the antics of my mind, I see that what is inside of me is always leaking out and coloring the space I move around in. I have no idea whether things outside of me change their attitudes or not. All I can really see out there is myself.

12

Zen Practice:
Meditations on Meditation

Meditation is not mysterious. There is no deep trick to it, no esoteric secret. It is not about repeating foreign words to yourself, or putting yourself in a trance, or seeing visions. It is not even about having a perfectly clear mind. In meditation, you watch what your mind does. You watch it as you would watch a rather difficult person with whom you're going to be working on a major project — and this is, of course, the actual situation: the project is your life, and you're stuck with your mind for a partner.

To meditate you sit on a round black cushion called a zafu, in a cross-legged position (if you can manage it), with a blank white wall before your eyes. You can also meditate anywhere else you happen to be. All it requires is a certain detaching. I often feel as if a noisy machine is rampaging around in my head, and I am tied to it with a chain, being tumbled along behind. The movement of meditation is like unlinking the chain. The machine continues to career around, but I am not dragged along. I observe.

These are some observations:

1

In the car driving up to the mountains I aim to keep my mind still. I think of the stream of thoughts as a wavering line of smoke that comes up from a candle. It is exceedingly delicate, subject to the slightest influence. I almost have to hold my breath to keep it still. Any flick from the outside world will move it — the car wheels going over a bump and making a rhythm that reminds me of a song that reminds me of the time when that song was popular, which reminds me of what was happening then . . . and I'm lost. Even without any outside stimulus, if my attention wanders for a second, my mind will start moving of its own accord. It will take off in any of its favorite directions, most of which lead either to pain or to a feverish excitement, a fragile agitated state of cheer.

It seems that the intrinsic nature of this unconscious thinking, what Joanna Field called "blind thought," is to lead down into suffering. Blind thought is the ego convincing itself of its reality and growing stronger and stronger. And the stronger it grows, the more in control, the more it pulls you down with it into the pit. This is its nature: when given its head, blind thought is like a horse returning to the barn. It makes you depressed and angry in unexplainable ways, and it creates the feeling of constant intangible discontent that we pin on one thing or another, but which can't really be ascribed to any of them because it is there no matter what, under everything — all the achievements and possessions and pleasures.

Consciousness leads up and out. Consciousness is not plastering a different state on top of unconsciousness. It is stopping the headlong forward rush of unconscious thinking. Just stopping, so that it becomes possible to see what's there instead. And stopping becomes desirable only when you have seen the nature of unconscious thought, when you've seen how devious it is and how unscrupulous, how it will stop at nothing to seize your attention, how it wants to be the master, how it operates *by itself*, without your permission or effort. It deceives you into thinking that it's something you are doing on purpose, and our language colludes in this by calling it thinking. We say, "I'm thinking about such and such," when really it would be more accurate to say, "Thoughts about such and such are tearing through my head." That's why meditation is so valuable. Without it, you don't see the character of this kind of "thinking," and so you don't have any particularly strong motive to do anything about it. You don't see how it is undermining you, how it is sapping your energies and carrying you off like the current of a river.

2

I used to think that if I went to a meditation retreat and did it right I would feel wonderful afterward — full of light and clarity and joy. I never did feel that way, so I thought I must have been meditating wrong. Now I seem at last to have gotten what the Guide has been saying all along — that when you meditate you just look at what's going on, just watch it. What's going on may be tension, anxiety, depression, a tendency to fall asleep. The point is to keep as close an eye on it as you can. There's no guarantee that doing this will stop whatever's going on. After meditation, I may feel as tense and awful as I did before. Or I may not.

3

When I try again and again to still my mind and thoughts come and grab me anyway, I say, "I can't do this." The Guide says, "We focus on all the times we fail and say, 'See? I can't do it,' instead of seeing the times when we *are* doing it. We say, 'I can't do it, I can't seem to concentrate, maybe if I did this or that, it's because of that or the other'. . . . Shut up," she says. "Stop all that."

Okay.

4

There is the silence in which everything exists, and then there is the noise in my head that I have come to take as the natural background to my life. It has occurred to me that perhaps the trick is to begin to see the silence as the background and the noise as moving across it. The silence, the plain existence of things, is what is real, and the thoughts are clouds.

5

My nose was running during the evening meditation. A drop hovered near the tip, and felt as if it was about to fall. This was a source of distraction and distress. I did not let myself put up my hand and wipe the drop away. My feeling about it seemed out of proportion to the scale of the problem. It wasn't painful; it wouldn't have been embarrassing if it *had* dripped because no one would have seen it. And yet it was hard to notice it as a sensation without feeling as though I could not stand it another second.

6

I have come to recognize what I call the fake urgency. It appears as soon as the bell rings and the silence falls. It is an itch on the side of my nose, one of those little tickles that feels as if a tiny moth is turning somersaults on my skin. Or it is the catch in my throat that *must* be cleared, or I will choke to death. It sucks up all my attention immediately. How am I going to live with this tickle on my nose or this frog in my throat for the next thirty minutes? I *could* scratch; I *could* clear my throat. But I will not, I won't move unless it is absolutely unbearable; this is my discipline for myself.

What I have finally learned is that the itch and the frog are fakes. I think of them as beings, imps of some kind, whose aim is to goad me. They know that to be effective they must appear *after* the bell, not before. Their voices are intensely persuasive: I am going to bug you beyond endurance, they say, unless you take care of me. It isn't true. All that's required — and it isn't easy, but it's possible — is to turn my attention resolutely away from them. Focus on my knee, which is untroubled; focus on my back, which hurts in its familiar undemanding way. After a few moments thoughts start to arise, and I am whisked in various directions and get involved in the motion that goes back and forth between thought and silence, and at some point I notice in a small faintly interested way that the itch, or frog, has gone.

How nice if I could do this with larger urgencies: an agony of embarrassment sweeps over me because I have said something gauche. I turn my attention to my knee, keep it there for a minute or two, and embarrassment evaporates. This is advanced work.

7

Form any relationship with the voice in the head besides indifference and you are lost. Which means: do not indulge the tunes in your head and the constant thoughts, and don't fall into despair about them either. Just notice.

8

The voice in the head. I can hear it better and better. It always has a comment to make, usually a rather inane one. If I see a gorgeous sunset, it either says, "What a gorgeous sunset!" or it makes up writerly similes about it. It says how it feels about everything — food, jobs, weather, people. It is always reporting its achievements or its troubles. It is defensive — gets into arguments all the time, tends to be sarcastic. It is fearful and tells horrible stories about what might happen. I can begin to see that I am not this voice but something that *includes* this voice. It is true that the silence and solitude of Middlefield make me aware of this in a way I am not in my regular life.

13

Windows

We went shopping for windows. This meant going to places with warehouses in back and store-like areas in front where doors and windows were on display. It was odd to see doors and windows standing alone, not in walls. They became obstructions in space rather than openings, the exact opposite of what they usually are. You had to go around them instead of through them.

The friendly salesman showed us sliding aluminum windows in brown, black, and silver; large-paned windows with grids slapped onto them to make them look like small-paned windows; plain wood windows drenched in preservatives; wood windows coated with vinyl; and vinyl windows without any wood in them at all. All these windows were highly technical. They came with brochures explaining how the chemicals and vinyl made them impervious to drought, rot, and warp, though not explaining why the vinyl coating would not, after a while, begin to crack and split, making the windows shabby in a way that couldn't be repaired by a simple coat of paint. We asked the salesman to figure up how much a plain wood window, about four feet by six feet, without vinyl, would cost. "Nine hundred forty-six dollars and twelve cents," he said.

I fell into a foul mood. It wasn't just that this seemed like a lot of money. Even if I'd had the money, I wouldn't have wanted to spend it on the windows I saw in that store. The problem was, they were ugly, cheap-looking, ill-crafted, phony, dishonest windows, and the thought of putting them into what I hoped would be a simple, beautiful, at-one-with-the-environment house filled me with despair. Sylvia, who was better at keeping things in perspective, did not get as worked up about the windows as I did, but she disliked them, too.

It is a serious matter, beauty. I think the skin-deep definition is wrong. A truly beautiful object is not likely to be pretty on the outside and ugly underneath ; wholeness is necessary to beauty. When you look around at the world — at the things that occur naturally in the world, that is — you don't see much that's ugly. Water, trees, flowers, rocks, fish, birds — all are astoundingly beautiful. If you take a couple of steps back from your human bias, less immediately appealing things such as cactus plants and boa constrictors and sinkholes full of boiling mud are also beautiful. Whoever made the ten thousand things of the world (let's imagine for the moment that someone did) paid close attention to the fine points. No detail has been sketched in carelessly, or left out in the interests of time. Why is nature like this? Why would any craftsman be so zealously attentive to every tiny detail?

The philosopher Krishnamurti says that attention is love. That makes perfect sense to me. This world, which is so beautiful, which displays infinite attention to detail, must grow out of love. Then does ugliness come from lack of love? Certainly one reason we have ugly aluminum windows is that the manufacturers can make a lot of them easily and cheaply. The only love in that is the love of money. Look behind nearly every ugly thing and you will find that it was made with a dead indifference, or with the hope of gain. Making a beautiful thing takes time, attention, and care. That's what I wanted in the windows, so they would match the rest of the house.

I explained the problem to the Guide. "Why don't you make your own windows?" she said. I smiled tolerantly, thinking this must be a joke. I have no skill at woodworking. Once I tried to make a toilet paper holder with a flat piece of wood, a dowel, and a drill, and the result had to go into the firewood pile. But she meant her suggestion seriously, and I could see no alternative. Maybe, I thought, Sylvia would be good at woodworking. She had made our outdoor shower floor, after all; and she'd done other things that, while not exactly carpentry, were more or less in the construction field: she'd painted the entire outside of the house one summer, all by herself, and she'd installed a drip-watering system in the garden. This was evidence of a sort of handyman inclination, I thought. "Do you think you might have a talent for window-making?" I asked her. She didn't know. She looked doubtful. But she was willing to give it a try.

We signed up for a woodworking class at the local high school. June, another member of the Center, enrolled with us. She had some experience with wood, having made meditation benches for meditators whose legs would not fold.

The class was held in a drafty box of a building with barn doors on the front and machines inside that had the look of dinosaurs, their jaws and fangs frozen in the moment before they closed down on their prey. Sawdust covered the floor, and the place smelled like oil and hot metal. The teacher explained each machine and told us how to work it. I fought a desire to go right home. Each time he turned on one of the machines it made a hideous screech or roar or whine. You had to wear earplugs against the noise, and then you couldn't hear what anyone was saying. Many people in the class had taken it before. They were taking it again only to have access to these tools. They were making advanced things like laminated tabletops and cabinets and futon bases.

We told the teacher we wanted to make windows. He looked interested, in a skeptical way, and said we should go to the library to find books about windows, and also to a junkyard, where we could buy the sort of window we wanted and take it apart to see how it went together. We went to a salvage yard down by the railroad tracks, where the piles of junk were like a small mountain range, in the middle of which was a tiny shed, where an electric fan blew air on a fat man in overalls. From him we bought an old window that was just barely not falling apart.

To make a good window, you have to keep a visual image of the finished product in your head for constant reference. Otherwise you end up with pieces of wood that will fit together properly only if you turn them upside down or backwards. Sylvia had trouble with this. The image in her mind kept dissolving when she wasn't looking at it and reassembling itself in faulty ways. "I can't do spatial relationships," she said, after having drilled some holes in the wrong side of the frame. She confined herself mostly to tasks that did not require visualization, such as fetching the T-square from the tool closet.

My problem was with precision. It seemed to me that the smallness of the lines on the ruler between the quarter-inch marks was an indication of their lack of importance. I could not believe that something as tangible as carpentry could require that you deal with abstractions like five sixteenths or nine thirty-seconds. When the marks on the ruler seemed too small, I put my pencil line where my intuition told me it should go. The consequences of this technique were occasionally out of all proportion to its harmlessness, as when, for example, a hole and a peg missed each other by a sixty-fourth of an inch.

Once you've cut the pieces of the window, you have to put them together so that they are at exact right angles and stay that way rather than relaxing into parallelograms. This requires you to make joints where two pieces of wood come together. We studied joints in the books we'd found in the library. There's the mortise and tenon joint, the rabbet joint, the dovetail joint. On paper they look simple. You make a sort of peg on this piece of wood and a hole for it to fit into on that piece. In practice this is hard because you need special tools to do it. You need a router with a certain kind of bit, a drill with a certain kind of jig, a saw with a certain kind of blade, and our workshop was equipped with only one of each of these.

We spent quite a bit of time in wood class waiting for someone else to finish using the tool we wanted. Someone who was making forty-two slats for his laminated tabletop always got to the saw ahead of us. The floor of the wood shop was cement; standing on it for two hours made my back hurt, but there was nothing to sit on except the stools at the work tables, which were occupied almost all the time. Also, of course, you couldn't have much of a conversation while you waited for the saw or the router, because there was too much roaring and screeching going on. My clearest memory from those evenings of woodworking is of Sylvia leaning against a table, with her arms folded, wearing ear protectors that were like large old-fashioned headphones and looking wanly down at the sawdust on the floor.

Wood class lasted eight weeks. By the end of that time we had measured and cut four boards for the frame of our first window, a practice window that was to be a model for the real windows we would make later. We had drilled holes in these four boards and put them together with dowels, an easier method than making the joints, and the result was the final product of our two months of work: a nice wooden rectangle.

We also learned many valuable things. Sylvia and I learned that we disliked woodworking a great deal and were not good at it, and June learned that she liked it well enough to volunteer to make our windows for us, which she did, lavishing upon them time, attention, and care. They were beautiful. This is how learning woodworking solved the window problem, proving the Guide right, as she so often is.

14

Electricity

This was to be a real house, not a rustic cabin. We wanted a place where we could live — light and spacious, beautiful and clean. Of course we would need electricity. We came to the point in our plans where it was time to figure out how to get it. The first step was to call Pacific Gas and Electric and find out the procedure. We figured they would string a wire up here somehow, and pretty soon we'd be hooked up and could start plugging things in.

I called and explained our situation. "You have to tell us where the nearest power line is," the man said. "Then we can figure out how much it will cost to run the line from there onto your property."

So Sylvia and I walked down the creek road, across the creek, out the gate, and toward the nearest house, which belonged to the rancher who owned the pasture land bordering the Center's property. Out in the fields, a good distance from the road, we spotted one of those tall skeletal electrical towers. Power lines connected it to another tower farther back toward the hills and another one beyond that. This tower in the middle of the pasture appeared to be the end of the line. The cables looped up to it and stopped. What was the distance from there to our site? We studied our topographical map. It looked like something under half a mile. I called PG&E with this information.

"The cost is six dollars a foot," said the PG&E man. There was a short silence while he punched his calculator. "To bring the line onto your property," he said, "would come to about twelve thousand dollars."

This was, you could say, a severe electric shock. We did not have twelve thousand extra dollars. We scolded ourselves. Sensible people would have done some research before buying a piece of property miles from nowhere. They would have looked into questions of water and roads and electricity. We had not been sensible; we had just leapt blindly forward, and this was the consequence: trouble. What good is a house with no electricity? I pictured sitting in the dim evening at a manual typewriter, and reading by the light of a smoky propane lamp, and keeping food in a cooler full of melting ice. I thought maybe we shouldn't build a house after all.

This was one of those times when what appears to be a disaster turns you in an interesting direction that you would never otherwise have known about. The universe throws something at you that seems like a problem and then waits to see if you're clever enough to find the blessing in it. In this case Michael, our architect, was the one who was clever enough. "Photovoltaics," he said. "Electricity from the sun. You should look into it." He told us that Gary Snyder, the poet whose Ring of Bone Zen Center was not far away, had a photovoltaic system that supplied his electricity. Snyder, he said, was a friend of his. He'd write and ask him about it.

Gary Snyder sent back a swarm of technical information. "I'm doing this," his letter said, "on a Mac Plus that is powered by two Arco M-12 panels that are charging one set of Trojan L-16 batteries with 300 AH storage, and — though the lights are straight DC — the computer & printer need AC so that's done with a 1200 W Trace inverter." We didn't know what all this meant, but it sounded encouraging. Gary Snyder wasn't sitting in the dark with a manual typewriter. He went on: "This is in Allen Ginsberg's little house that I use for an office. Our main house has a larger array that runs all the lights, the tapedeck, and Masa's [his wife's] computer and printer, and occasional vacuuming." They didn't have enough power to run a refrigerator or freezer, he said; those were propane. But if you put in a big enough photovoltaic system you could do anything you wanted. "I figure mine paid for itself in about eight years," he said. "Whatever electricity I get now is all free."

Free electricity from the sun! No bills from the power company! We loved the idea. We wrote off for information and started reading up on the technology. The catalogs showed pictures of mobile homes and mountain houses with tiers of glass panels on their roofs, slanted toward the sun. Captions underneath the pictures told how many watts the panels produced and what appliances they would operate. We went around the house making a list of all our electric appliances, figuring out the watt hours they used every day, and considering which of them were likely to be on at the same time (the lights and the computer, for instance, but probably not the blender, the hairdryer, and the vacuum cleaner). We learned about inverters, which change the direct current that comes straight from the batteries into alternating current. We learned the term "power grid," which is what everybody in civilization takes for granted. You run a wire from your house a few feet out to the street and you're connected to the power grid, the vast network of electricity racing along wires all over the country. I had never heard of the power grid before, because it's like the air you breathe. You don't have to think about it until you are in a place where there isn't any.

It wasn't going to be cheap to get power from the sun. The system we settled on would cost around five thousand dollars. Still, it was less than half the price of connecting to the power grid, and once it was going we would have no bills. We put in our order: eight panels, a frame to hold them, four batteries to store the electricity, and an inverter to change some of it to AC. (The lights, we decided, would be DC: it's cheaper and more efficient.)

A few weeks later, huge cardboard boxes arrived via UPS. We toted them up to the site and tore them open. There was technology inside, rather intimidating but beautiful. The panels were a foot wide and four feet long, rectangles of deep blue glass with fine turquoise lines running under the surface in a geometrical design. The batteries were the size of gas cans, and so heavy that one person could barely heave them off the ground. The inverter looked like a stereo receiver: it had knobs and switches on it, and dials with letters in fine print. Instructions came with this collection of equipment, and also cables, wires, and bolts. We started to read. It was interesting but alarming, too. There were warnings about hooking things up wrong and wrecking the system, and warnings about touching the panels once they were working and experiencing "lethal electric shock."

Greg helped us set it up. I should say, really, that Greg set it up and we helped. What we had to do first was build a shed whose roof would hold the panels. We put the shed in a small clearing to the east of the house, where the sun would hit the panels in the morning and shine on them until midafternoon, when it would sink behind the trees. Inside the shed, which was made of plywood and lit by two windows bought from a salvage yard, Sylvia and I built a box for the batteries, designed so that it was like a bench in the corner. Instead of having a lid that lifted up, the box had two doors on the front side that opened out from the center and revealed the batteries within. This way, when you wanted to open the box, you didn't have to clear off whatever you'd put on the top, and — more important — you could drag the batteries out the front when you had to remove them, rather than having to heave them up and over the side. We were proud of our box. I took a picture of Sylvia sitting by it, smiling, her arm flung across it, in the way a parent might pose with an arm around a child's shoulders.

Our power system was complete: on the roof, the eight panels in their tilted frame, soaking up energy from the sun; inside the shed, on the wall beside the battery box, a gauge with a red, yellow, and green dial to tell us whether the power was high or low; on a shelf beneath the gauge, the inverter, steadily humming; and in the box in the corner, the four batteries quietly storing up electricity and doling it out again in small useful amounts.

One night soon after we'd set all this up, I took a gooseneck lamp and my Macintosh computer up to the shed. I put the lamp on a shelf I'd made by nailing a two-by-four between two studs, and I spread a blanket over the battery box and set my computer and myself upon it. I plugged in the cords. I turned on the switches. The yellow lamplight streamed out, the computer pinged. Its smiling Macintosh face appeared on the screen, touchingly unaware that it was coming to life in a toolshed and being powered by the sun.

I started typing. Through the open door of the shed I could see the faded remains of the orange sunset, and the trees black against the sky. The leaves of the bush by the shed door were lit by my lamp. Moths fluttered in and flapped against the computer screen. A daddy-longlegs crawled down the plywood wall. Outside the crickets hummed on a long steady note, and inside the inverter buzzed a long steady buzz.

It seemed a great marvel, this juxtaposition of dark untouched nature and high technology. No light but the moon and stars had ever shone in this woods at night before — except for the light of campfires in the distant past. In our times, there had been only the flicker of a propane lamp and an occasional flashlight beam poking into the dark. And now all of a sudden came a flood of light and the tapping of computer keys.

I saw myself as if I were looking from high above, in one of those movie shots that takes in a whole wide landscape. First we see the vast encompassing darkness, the tree-covered hills like huge heads of black cauliflower — and in the middle of it, a glow of light. The camera zooms slowly in, the light gets bigger, and then we see the small crude building with the slant of panels on top, and the light shining out from the two windows. The door creaks open, blown by a soft night breeze, and inside in the incongruous brightness is a woman in jeans and a T-shirt, typing intently on a computer. Then we switch our view to the outside, we focus in among the branches of the trees and the clumps of grass on the ground. We see the birds taking their heads out from under their wings, and the mice standing momentarily still on their haunches with their tiny front paws dangling and their button eyes round and wary. What is this tappety-tappety noise? What is this light coming out where there never was any before? They can't comprehend it; it must be some kind of miracle.

15

Looking into the Future

One winter morning, when Sylvia and I were at home in town, we stood talking in the middle room, which was where we kept our information about the house. I have forgotten what we were discussing. We may have been leafing through one of the file folders labeled Electric, Plumbing, Septic Tank, Phone, Well, Rammed Earth. We may have been talking about roofing materials, or looking up the phone number of the well diggers, or inspecting my little cardboard house model. Suddenly, apropos of nothing, Sylvia said, "I'll never live to see this house."

It was a remark that seemed to drop through the ceiling like a stone, random as a meteor strike. If she had said it a different way, it could have been a facetious comment on the slowness of the process: "This house is going to take more than a lifetime to build." But no humor sounded in her words; neither did any note of dread. The statement had no special emotional quality to it at all, and was therefore so odd that neither of us responded. We looked at each other in some surprise and mystification, and then looked away and went on talking.

In early April, we spent a weekend at Middlefield, where the lupine and buttercups had sprung up in the new green grass. Taking a tape measure and a ball of string to our clearing, we measured out the lines of the house, picturing it for the first time in its precise location. It seemed large; its kitchen door would open right into a thicket of toyon and scrub oak. We got out the chainsaw, and all day, in the unseasonable heat, we chopped through the thick tangle of branches until we had backed up the woods a little and made some breathing space.

That night, as she undressed, Sylvia felt something under her left arm. It got in the way of motion, as though her sleeve had wadded up. But it wasn't her sleeve, it was a lump in her armpit. "Feel this," she said. I pressed it gingerly. The lump was hard, and when I pushed it seemed to move under her skin. "You've pulled a muscle holding the chainsaw up too high," I said. "Something has popped in there." She nodded. The shadow of the old fear swept over us — this lump was under her left arm, the same side as that cancerous mole years before. Surely that was a coincidence. If five years passed without a recurrence, the doctors had said, you can be pretty sure you're all right. It had been five and a half years.

The day after the chainsawing, a purple bruise spread out around the lump and ran like a streak of watercolor down Sylvia's side. We were relieved to see it. A bruise spreads out around an injury, doesn't it? Not around a tumor. Just the same, she went to the doctor to have it checked. He didn't say, as we had expected him to, "Oh, yes, an injury, nothing to worry about." He said, "This is a lymph node, and it's too hard, too big. I want you to see the surgeon."

A week later I sat with the Guide in the waiting room of the surgery center, staring at the pages of old *Time* magazines, tearing little strips of skin off my fingers. In the room down the hall, where Sylvia lay on a table anaesthetized, wearing a paper nightgown, the surgeon was slicing into the lump under her up-raised arm. He would take out a piece of tissue and send it in a car to the hospital lab, where the technicians would analyze the sample and phone back the results. By the time he emerged from the operating room, he would know whether it was melanoma or not. If it was, we would face a grim prospect: Melanoma, once it begins to spread, is almost always fatal.

We waited and waited. People drifted through, walking slowly, accompanied by relatives who held them by the elbow. The chipper voice of the receptionist sounded in the background. The Guide and I talked in snatches now and then: she said that if she were to go to Europe it would be to see the architecture. That's all I remember of our conversation. I looked at my knees, at my gray jeans. I looked through the glass doors at the spring day, clear with clouds blowing. After a long time the doctor came out, wearing his baggy light green suit, his mask hanging under his chin. He squatted in front of us, put his elbows on his knees, laced his fingers together, and looked up.

"It's melanoma," he said. "We didn't even need to send the tissue to the lab. It was black. The color of your socks."

The days after that were like days from a different life, days from someone else's life that had mistakenly been inserted into mine. Plans for the house, which had been moving steadily for-ward for so long, stood still and faded into the background, like a movie stopped in mid-reel by a failed projector. What was im-mediate took over: the bag attached to Sylvia's side, from which fluids had to be drained every few hours; the pain pills to be taken on schedule; the movies to be rented from the video store to oc-cupy evenings that would otherwise fill up with dread. We talked very little. I cried. Sylvia didn't. She said she was not afraid.

People called and stopped by, bringing flowers, saying fear-ful, tentative things, trying to be reassuring. "You'll be all right," they said, and were disconcerted when Sylvia told them that she was all right now. She was strangely calm. In her place, I knew I'd be protesting wildly. I would feel caught in a nightmare, and I would thrash and wail at the horror of it, longing to wake up. But she felt she had been given fair warning and made good use of it. She said it was as if she had had a tap on the shoulder five years before: "Hey," says Death, and crooks a beckoning finger. "Are you ready?" She leaps back, she's jolted horribly awake. No! Not yet! and makes right then a turn, inside herself, toward a different life.

She hadn't stopped in her tracks and replaced all her old activities with new ones. It was more as if she'd allowed a door to open that had been closed, and what had been outside that door, waiting patiently on the step, began to come inside — Zen practice, the Guide, the land in the mountains. She had already quit her job by then, before she knew about the cancer. It was time, she thought, to get along on less money and do more of what she loved. In her new leisure hours, she worked at home in the garden, pruning and tending. She offered her services at a nearby stable, where she could be in a world familiar to her from childhood — trodden hay, the smell of manure, the soft nudging noses of horses. Mastering her aversion to technology, she learned the rudiments of my computer and began to write, mostly about her spiritual practice.

These were the changes you could see, the ones that appeared in the outside world. Inside, her change came in realizations, not blinding flashes, but understandings that emerged into her awareness in a way that I imagine to be like the gradual development of a Polaroid photograph. She came home one afternoon, sometime during those five years, and said that — though she knew it was going to sound corny — she had realized while driving along the expressway that she was love. "I am love," she said, with a happy simplicity, as if she had discovered some unexpected and interesting fact about herself, as if she were saying, "I am part Cherokee." It was the same with the conviction that she was all right, in some essential way that disease could not touch. She knew it, rock solid.

"Not that I *want* to die," she said. "I like my life." But she wasn't going to beat her fists against death, or cower in the face of it.

Besides, maybe she wouldn't die. Remissions were not absolutely unheard of, the doctors told us. Sometimes the disease retreated and waited for years before flaring up again. "It's unpredictable," they said over and over, this being one of their few certainties. "It can stay dormant for years." They held out frail twigs of hope for us to cling to. Radiation could slow the growth of tumors, if they were in the right place. Certain drastic experimental treatments could offer a ten percent chance of at least temporary recovery, in exchange for weeks in the intensive care unit of the hospital. I felt sorry for the doctors who offered us, so shamefacedly, so deferentially, this information. They seemed, although they must have had much practice in delivering bad news, in need themselves of comfort and reassurance.

After a week or so we went to the beach to talk about What Now. Until then we had shied away from the subject of the house, but it was looming at us; it needed discussing. We had made a special occasion for our talk. The air was clear and bright, and a ferocious wind was blowing. It was too cold to get out of the car; we sat in the front seat, looking out at the opaque green water frothing with whitecaps. We had our talk. It was not a long, intense, convoluted talk; we had less to say, or less energy to say it, than I had expected. The sensible course, we agreed, was to go on with the house as planned, simplify as much as possible to cut costs, and build as much as we could before we ran out of money and before the cancer came back, if it was going to. But the joy of house planning had drained away. I felt almost guilty about it, as if the house were a child who has been the center of attention for a long time and then is suddenly forgotten, left alone at the end of the hall, because something urgent has arisen that must be attended to. It's not her fault. She waits, forlorn and reproachful.

Spring turned into early summer, and the house plans accumulated. Before long, we would arrive at the starting line, and at the word go, workers would climb into trucks and head up dirt roads to our clearing. The backhoe would gouge out long gashes in the ground, the piles of dirt would rise, men's voices would shout instructions, and the house would begin to go up. And still, in our minds, in spite of the wan agreement we had come to at the beach, the questions rocked back and forth, unanswered. Should we build? Should we take on this immense project at this precarious time? For Sylvia the decision was too big, and at the same time irrelevant, hard to focus her mind on. I was the one who had to decide.

Michael called, wanting to know what was happening. Proceed, I said, feeling fake, as if the project had already been canceled and I was keeping it a secret from him. I didn't know what else to say.

In May, we were at Middlefield again. The man with the towering truck came to put the well in, and the gas company arrived with the propane tank. We looked around our site, we talked, but our talk faltered. "The truth is," said Sylvia, "I have no energy for building this house."

I made up every possible future and a solution to go with each one. Maybe the surgery had eradicated the cancer. In that case, we'd want the house. Maybe the surgery had eradicated all but one cell, and that cell would lie around doing nothing for years. Why not, during those years, be living in this house? Or maybe the cancer would come back soon. The question was, how soon? Would there be time between now and then to build? Was building the best way to spend that time? And if we built the house and Sylvia died, then what? Did I want to live alone in the mountains, next door to a Zen monastery? I didn't know. I wasn't sure who I would be if Sylvia died; we had been together nearly ten years. I couldn't find any solid ground on which to base a decision.

And then one evening, when we had returned home and I was in the kitchen making dinner, the obvious solution dawned on me. It had taken me an awfully long time to see it. If it had been a person, it would have been yelling at me for weeks from its invisible dimension, red in the face with exasperation at my denseness. Distress, I suppose, had made me stupid. But now at last I had hit on the way to have everything — a simpler, shorter project, a smaller expenditure of money, and a house, too: we would build just the office, the one Michael had drawn as a separate building. It was small, but it would have all the conveniences — running water, electricity, heat, a bathroom. Some day, if Sylvia lived and circumstances favored it, we could build the big house. But for now, we'd table that project. This was the perfect answer, we both agreed. All the tension of that hanging decision dissipated.

We could go forward, operating as though we had no idea what might be coming and were sensibly preparing for any eventuality. We acted as though she had a fifty-fifty chance: she might live, she might not. We collected factual evidence. The CAT scans taken once a month showed no new melanoma; the doctor said the surgery might possibly have gotten all the cancer cells; the lump under her arm, blasted by radiation four times a week, was indisputably shrinking. Sylvia was tired a lot, but that could be the radiation, or it could be anxiety. She felt a shortness of breath, as the summer went on, a faint constriction in the lungs that she noticed when she went up hills, but that could be anxiety, too, or maybe the smogginess of the air. Her appetite was small, but when you're anxious you don't have much appetite. Besides, it was summer, it was hot, and no one eats when it's hot. We don't know, we just don't know, we said. Anything could happen.

And on another level, we did know. The startling sentence that had appeared that day in the middle room came back to me one afternoon as we were walking down to the creek. She remembered it, too. We spoke of it cautiously, respectfully, recognizing it for a wonder. Sylvia had been as bewildered by it as I was; she'd had no idea where it came from. Though we didn't say so out loud, I think for both of us those words had an oracular power beside which the facts seemed frail.

There must be a dimension in which the future is as accessible as the past. I imagine our ordinary reality as a sphere that turns within other spheres and can be pierced sometimes, so that we see briefly through the hole into a larger more inclusive reality. This is why you can know and not know something simultaneously: one kind of knowing belongs to our own sphere, the other belongs to the sphere outside ours. We have no skills for grasping that kind of knowledge. It is like a puff of air or a piece of transparent jelly; you can feel its presence, but you can't see it, you can't say what it is. It's wordless, though words may be a sign of it. Sylvia didn't say to herself, after that moment in the middle room, "I know now that I'm going to die." The knowledge didn't translate itself into an ordinary fact, on the same level as "I have a tumor under my arm." There is no place for that kind of knowing in the kind of reality in which we live our everyday lives, as there is no place in mathematics for a tree or the word "apple."

I understand this because of an experience I once had, a similar glimpse beyond our sphere. In content it was utterly trivial: at a conference — something to do with book publishing — I went to a session in which the author of a children's book was going to speak. We had all written our names on slips of paper as we came in; a copy of the author's book, the moderator announced, would be awarded at the end of the talk. The author stood up and spoke. I don't remember what she looked like or what she said, but all through that hour, the awareness that I was going to win that book sat in some closed pocket of my mind. I did not put it into words. I hardly acknowledged its presence, but I knew it was there, the way you can know that someone has entered a room even though you neither see nor hear him. At the end of the hour, when the speaker sat down and the winner was announced, I was not surprised to hear my name.

16

Zen Practice:
There Is Nothing to Fear

■

There is nothing to fear, said the Guide in that first encounter. But how can this be? Surely she is wrong. There is so much to fear.

There is the rapist in the bushes at the park, and the lost soul with drugs in his blood and a gun in his pocket. There is the elevator that sticks between floors when the earthquake strikes, and the missiles waiting underground for their signal, and the disease that begins as a bump or a spot and spreads out its greedy, deadly fingers.

Count up the things to be afraid of; they are endless: you can be afraid of catching your arm in the gears of a machine, or of running over a child that darts in front of your car, or of falling out of the sky in an airplane. You can be afraid of getting old, or dying too soon, or losing the people you love. You can be afraid of pain.

Don't tell me there is nothing to fear.

I'm an expert at fear: if catastrophes are scarce, my imagination supplies them. All my journeys have been preceded by plane crashes or car wrecks. I have spent hours fighting off murderers, trapped under the rubble of fallen skyscrapers, and lost in the bad sections of cities. In the summer of 1962, a nuclear inferno blazed in my head night after night. I know what there is to be afraid of.

Here is the strange thing: Sylvia is not afraid. She is the one with the black cells multiplying inside her, the threat of pain hanging over her, and the end of her life, which should be fifty years away, striding toward her from around the corner. But she is staying where she is. She is not moving outside the border of the moment, in which she is very much alive. Things as they are occupy her attention: the phone call to the doctor, the pill to be taken, the letters to write to friends across the country. Her mind, especially in the evenings, tries to start up its alarms — but she quiets it as well as she can. She draws her attention in close.

I send mine out in all directions, into a thousand futures, all of them terrible futures in which I will be unhappy. My thoughts swirl around faster and faster, making a black storm in my head so fierce and uncontainable that it darkens the air around me, obscuring what is happening now. It is true that what I am imagining is not real, at least not yet. But it *could* be real, any one of these futures could be real, and am I not fending them off by creating them ahead of time, so as to get them under control, so as to be prepared for what's coming?

A few times, a frightening event has erupted into my life rather than just into my mind. A big earthquake occurred once, and I stood clutching the frame of the kitchen doorway as plates slid off shelves and the furniture rocked. What I felt was different from the fear I am used to. My mind was shocked into silence. All my nerves were on edge, all my muscles came to attention, ready to deal with the emergency. I became a charged wire. In those seconds when something terrible actually was happening, I was not, in the way I ordinarily feel it, afraid.

Is this how it is for Sylvia? She is in the center of the disaster, and its roar and clatter are in her ears. She has no time for distractions. She deals with the concrete things that are the moment's requirements, and I deal with phantoms. She stays within the circle that outlines the present moment, and so for her the present moment fills up the entire universe. I leap from here to every other moment I can imagine, to a bad hour in the hospital, a night beside a bed, a time when I am alone . . . and so for me every moment, no matter what it contains, is filled with dread.

I've done this all my life, with one set of fears or another, and the waste of it is that what I dread never comes to pass, *never*. Most of what I fear doesn't happen at all; a bit of it happens, but in a form that barely resembles what I have imagined. Even my most detailed visions are wrong in some way and so do not prepare me for disasters any more than if I had never had them in the first place. What they do is keep me asleep, caught in my own dark mumblings and ramblings, while the solid, bright-colored things of each real moment slide by me unnoticed.

And when I see this I shake myself like someone trying to wake up from a drugged slumber. Look! Here I am once again in the midst of an earthquake, though it is one that will happen over months instead of seconds, and I need my wits about me and my hands free to do what's necessary. Time is passing. Every minute is different from the last minute, and who knows what will be in the next minute? I must not miss anything, but I will if I'm lost in my dreams of disaster. What I have called fear suddenly turns upside down and looks like a luxury I cannot afford. And so I remind myself, as often as I must, which is very often: hold still. Stay here. Put the groceries away, turn on the lights, get dinner ready. Try to remember: there is nothing to fear in this moment, and this is the only real moment there is.

17

The Summer of the House

■

Summer advanced, no cancer showed up, and house planning intensified. During the week, I sat at my desk at work, organizing things from a distance. The voices of Alma in the county building department, Lynn in the sanitation office, and Mike the Title 24 man became familiar to me, and mine to them. Are the plans approved yet? Have you got the forms I sent you? Did the engineering drawings turn up? I called contractors and asked them to come make bids on our job. I called businesses and asked about well pumps, wood stoves, and plumbing fixtures.

On the weekends, we drove to Middlefield and did up there — or tried to do — what I'd arranged from down here. Organizing things from a distance doesn't always work. Your voice reaches out in a long skinny tentacle across the countryside, but it can only grab hold of a few small, undependable scraps of information at a time. You call the county offices and talk to Alma, and when you call again Alma is on vacation and Thelma has taken over, who tells you something different. Mike the Title 24 man says, "This will be done in two weeks," and then you don't hear from him, and whenever you call, his answering machine beeps in your ear. The backhoe operator says he'll meet you at the bottom of your dirt road, and though you wait right there by the cattle guard for an hour, he does not show up. Somewhere in the three hundred miles between the town and the mountains, words are lost or rearranged in the air.

But little by little, haltingly, things got done. One weekend Jeff, the young backhoe operator, did show up at the bottom of the road, and we led him to the house site to make his estimate; another weekend Frank, the old backhoe operator, arrived to make his. Who do we go with, Jeff or Frank? We talked it over, we figured it out. Down by the creek we met the phone man and walked with him as he paced out the distance from the nearest line terminus to the edge of our property and then in, fighting through the blackberry bushes to a spot a certain number of feet from the road. "This is as far as the phone company will go," he said. "From here you have to take the wire up the hill yourself." Should we run it along the fence? Should we thread it through a pipe to keep the rats and squirrels from chewing on it? Housebuilding in a remote place keeps your mind occupied with these endless questions, so that other kinds of questions, ones you are just as glad not to think about, get pushed slightly to the side.

Back at home, we wrestled with the suburban traffic. The stores that sell what you need for a house are always on the widest, most swarming boulevards, six-lane streets with stop lights at every intersection, where traffic moves in jerks and rushes, and poisonous fumes from a thousand tailpipes mingle with the heat rising off the asphalt. These are the streets where you find the used car lots and the motels, and the big low stores with plate glass faces, where you can buy mattresses, refrigerators, sofabeds, and lawn furniture, and the flashy little shopping malls that sell quick haircuts and fast food. Very few of these establishments display their addresses in numbers readable from the street. You find the store you want by driving several miles past it until you come to a bank or a hotel whose number tells you you've gone too far, and then you turn around and go back. Impossible to turn left into the mall where your store is; you have to go up to the next light, wait there, listening to the rock music pounding out of the open window of the car beside you, and make a U. So you are frazzled when you arrive, and reduced in your ability to deal with the details that swarm like flies around every decision. Which shower will fit in the corner of the bathroom? Is it thirty-two inches from the door to the wall, or thirty-two and a half? How many inches from the stovepipe to the wooden beam?

Still, we managed to buy things. In a plumbing supply store that smelled of black pipe grease and dusty rubber, where shelves jammed with boxes of washers and knobs and pipe joints towered up to the ceiling, and customers walked sideways past each other through the narrow aisles, we bought a shower, the smallest one made, a white fiberglass shell with a glass door. At another place we found a water-saving toilet made in a Scandinavian country. Its flusher was a knob that sat on top of the oval tank like a cherry on a sundae, and its throat was not the fat throat of an ordinary toilet but a graceful S like the curve in an egret's neck. A melancholy man in a small store that had no parking lot of its own talked to us about catalytic converters and zero clearances, and we bought from him a tiny boxlike wood stove, an elegant stove with a glass door framed in brass, and a flat top on which you might set your coffeepot to boil water.

Between house expeditions, we went to doctor's appointments. When you have cancer, the doctors want you. They are all doing some sort of research that requires subjects. "See so and so," the oncologist said, "he's doing some work with chicken cells. It's an experimental program but it might be promising." "See so and so, too," the chicken cell doctor said, "there's a special diet program to strengthen cancer patients who are undergoing radiation, they might be able to take you." I think the person who gets the most out of these projects is the doctor who collects the information; but Sylvia followed up on a few of them, the ones that did not require hospital stays or treatments likely to make her feel miserable. In waiting rooms packed with glum uneasy people, we waited for appointments that began an hour after their scheduled time. A nurse would shut us into an examining room after a while, where Sylvia would take off her clothes, put on the pale blue paper gown they supplied, and sit on the end of the narrow table, shivering in the chilly air-conditioned air. The sight of her — her fine slender arms, her hands together in her lap, her pale shoulders — made the sadness swell up in my throat. When the doctor finally did arrive, she would answer his questions calmly, while I stuck my finger into a Kleenex and blotted the tears before they could fall down my face.

She felt all right. Now and then there was a faint pain in her chest, but nothing much. Little odd things went wrong with her, but whether they had to do with cancer or not no one could tell. She had hives, which she'd never had before, big red welts that appeared on her legs and back sometimes in the mornings and then faded. She had a bladder infection, another thing she'd never had. A few small bumps cropped up under her arm. Probably, we decided, they were scar tissue, hardening — not swollen lymph nodes.

We forged ahead with the house, coping with logistics, red tape, misunderstandings, and last-minute changes. By the end of the summer, everything was more or less ready to go. My sabbatical was about to begin — two months, which would be enough time, we figured, to get the walls up and put the roof over them. Then we could tack sheets of plastic across the door and window spaces, and during the winter the house could sit, closed against the weather, until building resumed in the spring.

Earnestly, with honest duplicity, if there can be such a thing, we made plans. What I mean is that we spoke brightly of the future as if we believed it was out there, while in some underground cavern of consciousness that other kind of knowing ran like a stream of black water. We kept in our hearts the picture of ourselves in the coming winter — two flannel-shirted figures under the cold gray sky, tossing branches into a great bonfire of brush and warming our hands around mugs of chocolate. How could so vivid a picture not be real? It was a piece of solid ground out there that we could make our way toward.

Step by step, the little house rose. First came the grading. We were building on a slope, not a steep one, but enough so that the backhoe had to cut out a big wedge of dirt to make a level place. You call this the house pad. (We learned construction lingo, a foreign language required for the project.) At the back, the house would nestle down into the ground; at the front, the ground would be level with the doorsill.

Into this level place the backhoe dug trenches outlining the shape of the house, a rectangle fifteen by eighteen feet — and in the trenches (which you call footings) the builders nailed together boxes out of thick planks and steel reinforcing bars (which you call *re*bar) to hold the cement of the foundation. The cement truck came lumbering up our narrow road, such a mammoth that we had to lop off tree branches to let it through. It stuck its chute out, the men grabbed the end of the chute and aimed it, and the trenches filled up with gray rock porridge.

The earth from the house pad and footings stood in a pile in the clearing. This was the material for the walls. The man on the tractor worked this pile constantly during the wall-building days, scooping up bucketfuls of it, dropping it through a sieve to sift out the rocks and sticks, and combing through it, back and forth, back and forth, while someone else tossed in the right amounts of cement and sand and sprayed on water with the hose.

When the dirt is fine and damp to the correct degree, the tractor scoops up a load of it, and the men climb up the side of the plywood box that has been built up from the foundation (you call this a wall form); then they shovel the dirt from the tractor bucket into the box. They put in about six inches and start up the pneumatic tamper, which looks like a jackhammer, only instead of having a blade on the end, it has a rubber thumper, a kind of mallet, that compacts the dirt until it rings when it's hit. Working the tamper rattles your skeleton and makes your flesh vibrate all over, so you feel like one of those cartoon characters with curved lines radiating out to indicate a massive shaking-up. I know this because I tried it for a while, but I was not strong enough to keep going for long.

One after another, they built the boxes for each section of wall and rammed in the earth. The finished walls were smooth and hard, a foot thick, and cool to the touch until they dried. They were a dark rich brown with small bits of color mixed in — green shreds of leaves, tan slivers of sticks and roots, gold scraps of grass, even a tiny gray bird feather here and there.

Beautiful, beautiful. I took pictures as it went up. The spindly oak tree near the front door made leaf shadows on the brown wall. I took a picture of that. I took a picture of the men, foreshortened against the blue sky, standing on top of the wall forms, their shoulders hunched, their arms making a straight rod down the center of their chests, holding onto the tampers. Later on I took a picture up through the wooden beams of the roof, and got Greg's knees and his hammer upraised in the air, ready to come down on the nail of the fine pale pine decking that would be the ceiling. A friend came to help for a few days and brought her video camera. She took a long rambling movie, in which I explain self-consciously what is going on; the men grunt and make jokes as they stir up the earth-and-cement mixture for the floor; and Sylvia drifts in around the edges, smiling, not saying much, looking thin in her dark blue polo shirt.

It was monstrously hot. We looked at the thermometer every morning and wondered if it had gotten stuck in the night. Even at dawn, the temperature was up around eighty. It went over a hundred every day. The heat filled all the space under the sky, like an invisible block of dome-shaped hot iron that pressed down on our shoulders when we went outside. Leaves were dry and gray, coated with dust, and dust rose in a cloud around our feet with every step. The skin behind our ankles turned brown and grimy, uncleanable, and our Achilles tendons were ridged with dryness like a reptile's neck. Everything was thirsty: birds stood on branches with their beaks gaping; a mouse crawled into the solar shower and drowned; lizards that came to the birds' water dish for a drink slipped in and lay there, limp and half-conscious. When the building noises stopped at lunchtime and at the end of the day, the woods were nearly silent, as if nothing had the energy to make more than small, infrequent sounds — ticking, crepitating, the tiny tap and scurry of lizard feet on dry leaves. In the distance, gunshots popped — it was hunting season.

We drank grapefruit juice out of the small cans that come in six packs, and mineral water with different flavors, and water out of our plastic water bottles. The water was the best — no carbonation to burn the throat, no sweet taste — but it heated up and took on the taste of plastic as the day went on.

I wore shorts and a tank top. Sylvia wore long pants and a light blue work shirt with the sleeves buttoned at the wrist, and she slathered sunscreen on her face and neck and hands. No cancer-causing ultraviolet rays could get to her. "You must be so hot!" I said, but she didn't care. "Don't want my white old legs showing anyway," she said.

The heat got to both of us, especially when our help wasn't needed on the house and we went back to cutting brush, or cutting firewood. Sweat gushed out of us. Our plastic goggles slipped and steamed. Over the chainsaw's roar, we shouted instructions at each other, but the ear protectors clamped over our ears muffled our voices. *What? What?* we yelled, on fire with irritation.

Turkey vultures circled high over the clearing. The feathers on the ends of their wings were like hyperextended fingers, curving up and backward. Their shadows swept across the dirt.

We alternated our time at the land that summer; sometimes we were there together, sometimes one of us was there and the other one at home in town. In the last part of September, I was there alone for two weeks. One morning I awakened to an eerie light in the sky, like the ominous mustard-colored light of an oncoming storm. Everything was very quiet, and small gray flakes fell like snow, settling on leaves and on the ground. The sun was a dim ball of fuzz; the air smelled of smoke. Somewhere not far away was a tremendous fire eating up the woods. I was afraid that day. I wanted to be someplace else. The sky leaned over me, dark and white, sifting and falling, whispering threats.

As time went on during that last week, the force of gravity seemed to grow stronger, pulling me into the ground and turning my feet to lead, and the air felt thicker, resisting me. I had to push against a hard current to move at all. Why am I so tired? I kept writing in my journal. Is it because I am so old? Is it because I am so lonely? I fought with the brush, and one day a stiff sharp branch sprang back at me spitefully and sliced the inside of my arm above the wrist where the skin is thin and tender. Blood popped out of the cut in beads, the beads blended together into a line, and the line flowed over my arm. I felt a great cruelty had been done, and that I had done it myself. Grief and guilt overwhelmed me, huge considering the smallness of the wound, and I had to put the clippers down, too sad to go on.

In the evenings, I drove out the monastery gate and up the road to the house of some neighbors who had let the Center put its phone in their garage. It was not really a garage, but a workshop, full of wide strong tables and woodworking tools with blades and teeth. The phone always had dust on it; so did the notebook where you wrote down what number you'd called and whether the call was business or personal. I called Sylvia to see how she was doing at home. How was the pain in her chest? The same, she would say, and we'd talk about smog, and go over all the reasons for the harmlessness of this symptom. She seemed far away and small. As I talked to her, I looked out the window at the pine trees roasting in the late afternoon sun, the air around them hazy with heat. Who would want to live here? I thought. This is a terrible place. We have made a mistake.

At the end of September, I left Middlefield to spend a weekend at home. I set out a few hours earlier than I had planned to and drove down out of the mountains and into the smog and traffic, happy to be away from the heat, happy at the prospect of surprising Sylvia. She was there in the kitchen when I walked in, talking on the phone to her father, telling him that the most recent set of x-rays had shown several small spots of cancer in her lungs.

18

Darkness and Light

The next three months were a long nightfall, winter and death sifting slowly down like twilight. Each day had more darkness in it than the one before, darkness that seemed to gather at both ends of the day, so that the light between grew briefer and dimmer.

At first Sylvia felt strangely well, for someone so ill. She was a little short of breath, a little weak; that was all. We continued our custom of taking a walk around two blocks in the evenings after dinner. But as time passed, her breath came harder, her strength diminished, and we walked more and more slowly. We had to stop often and rest, standing arm in arm under the streetlamps, looking at the black leafless trees with stars glittering coldly among their branches. After a while we shortened our walk to one block instead of two, and later we went only halfway down the street, then turned and came back. Her world was shrinking. After the beginning of November, when the radiation treatments ended, she did not leave the house again; by December, I could no longer persuade her even to take a turn around the living room.

The doctor ordered her an oxygen machine. It sat in the middle room, behind the closed door, which muffled a little the constant roar and thump it made as it sucked oxygen out of the air. A transparent plastic tube snaked under the door and down the hall, into Sylvia's bedroom, and up to a circle of tube that looped over her ears like glasses and blew air gently into her nose. All day, the machine chugged like an angry heart. You could feel it in the soles of your feet.

Her appetite waned. Only certain kinds of things appealed, white things and bland smooth sweet things. I made a list of them — pancakes, cottage cheese, canned peaches, mashed potatoes, custard. I carried the white tray with fold-down legs back and forth, bringing breakfast, lunch, and dinner, my old faith in the power of food sticking unreasonably with me. One by one, she stopped liking all the things on the list. She would sit with the plate in front of her on which I had arranged two soda crackers, a dab of cottage cheese, and two peach slices, and every five minutes or so she would take a tiny bite and then rest from the exertion of overcoming her repugnance. One day in mid-January she pushed the plate away and said, "No more solid food, ever again," and this turned out to be not just a wish but a statement of fact.

She didn't feel much pain — every now and then a twinge, somewhere in her left side. But the pain wasn't as bad as taking the pills against it. Better to have a pain than to risk the nausea that washed through her when she took the pills, or smelled ordinary food, or coughed too hard.

In the daytime she sat against a thick bolster of pillows, with a blue electric blanket over her legs. I read to her sometimes: *The Borrowers* and *The Cat Who Went to Heaven*. The Guide came, and she read to her, too — the *Heart Sutra*, the *Tibetan Book of the Dead*. Sometimes Sylvia watched the soap operas and the talk shows on TV, and when she tired of that she looked out the window at the yellow daisies bobbing in the rain. The sky was always gray. Robins hurled themselves at the pyracantha bush next to the glass door, squawking and shrieking, the impact of their bodies thumping the clumps of berries against the wall. In the afternoons, Sylvia slept, and as time went on her sleeps grew longer and deeper. She fell into sleeps that were like ocean abysses, from which she clawed her way back up into daylight, groaning. At night I listened for the sound of coughing down the hall from my room.

Death closed in from all directions, like the shutter of a camera. One day she said her legs felt as if they no longer belonged to her. They lay there on the bed in their gray sweatpants and white socks, and she looked at them with detachment, as if they were stuffed legs that someone had sewed on.

I asked her if she thought back over her life, and she said she did not. It was far away from her. It was not interesting. Only the moment in which she found herself held her attention.

She grew thin, but not terribly thin. She never looked ghastly, not even right at the end. Her skin tightened over her high cheekbones and her fine collarbones; her eyes looked larger, her forehead higher. She was not changed by the disease into a different person, only distilled by it down to her essence. No delirium scrambled her mind; she had no pain severe enough to require the drugs that would make her groggy and dull. She was herself until one Monday night, when a bad cough brought the pain stabbing into her lungs and the nurse came with a morphine device that attached to the bedside table and dripped fluid steadily from a tube into a needle in her arm. She lay on her back, her eyes open a slit, only the whites showing, and for three days she breathed through liquid as her lungs filled. Once she floated up into an otherworldly sort of consciousness. Her eyes opened and focused slightly, but not on us, and she spoke in a faraway voice. We bent to hear, holding our breath, and she said, with spaces between the words, "It's wonderful . . . I want you to know that it's all okay . . . thank you for everything you've done . . .

it's been nothing but wonderful, nothing but wonderful." She was on the threshold between two worlds, where she could see the one before her as clearly as the one she was leaving, and she had gathered the strength to call back to us, reassuring.

She worked hard in her last three days. Her heart was strong, not willing to give up easily. If the life force in her body had been a light, we would have seen it in those days concentrated in a shape like a pear — mouth, throat, heart, lungs, only the parts required to keep her breathing. It would have been a dense light, glowing like a red dwarf star, and falling inward. Her head and belly would have been full of shadows, and her limbs dark — feet abandoned, hands lying flat and limp on the blue cover of the bed. Her eyes filmed over, grew gummy and opaque — she had no use for them any more. Her mouth, half open, was only a hole to pull air through. The light drew in and in until finally, for hours on the last day, it was no more than a faint but stubborn candle flame, and she was a body being breathed, being pumped by whatever force it is in the universe that pumps breath through bodies. The breaths got rougher, halting, more and more shuddering and widely spaced. The last one came in the evening, a little after seven o'clock.

Then we followed the Buddhist way of caring for the dead. We sat with her for forty-five minutes. We washed and prepared her body, the Guide and I, dressed her in clean sweat pants and a T-shirt, wrapped her in a white sheet, so that only her face showed, with the sheet folded around it like a monk's hood. Under the bed we put branches of bay laurel and sage and pine, and we laid flowers on the bed around her. For three days, the house was open to those who wanted to come. And at the end of three days, on a rainy evening when all the people had gone, we brought in the pine casket that Greg had made and laid her in it. The next day we sat in the chapel adjoining the cemetery's crematorium and waited while the flames in the oven behind the altar burned casket, sheet, flesh, hair, and bone.

I was left with an emptiness where she had been. My mind wrestled with it but made no progress. None of my questions had answers: Where is she? How could she be gone? Is she still here somehow, watching me? Will she come again, in some other form? I can understand the appeal of reincarnation, which holds out the hope that each irreplaceable self will not be obliterated but moved along from one body to another, as if a life history were a long thread winding through the eons, with bodies strung along it like beads, always the same soul housed in one body after another. But I don't see how it can be so neat and linear as that; nothing else is. I imagine instead something more like a vast endlessly fertile jungle, in which everything is always reborn, but no one self ever occurs twice — the way leaves are reborn on a tree every spring, but the exact same leaf that was there last year never appears again. I do not expect to discover, twenty or thirty years from now, a person whose body is the new home for Sylvia's spirit.

I have tried to make death fit into my scheme of life, just as people have tried to do forever, picturing death as a shadowy land on the other side of a river, or a place in the sky full of harp music and white clouds — as if death were another country in life's geography. But I can't make this work. Death is *behind* life, it is the other side of life, not an aspect of life at all, as night is not an aspect of day. In my ordinary mode of operation I am so firmly embedded in life that I can do nothing with death but try to translate it into terms I understand. I look for an answer to it, as though it were a puzzle or a hard mathematical problem, and cling to the belief that if I could find such an answer, I might be comforted.

But there is no comfort, not for the part of me that wants to touch a solid shoulder again and hear the sound of a voice. That self never finds comfort, unless it can believe in a manufactured comfort — that we all go to heaven, that we will be reborn as higher beings, that our loved ones are still themselves only invisible, and will speak to us in their familiar voices if we knock on tables. The one who yearns for that comfort is inconsolable, always. But it has been suggested to me that my small self is held in the arms of another larger kind of being, made of life and death the way time on earth is made of night and day. If my struggling mind were to abandon its efforts, having been confounded at every turn, and collapse its walls so that for a moment it ceased to exist — then I might fall into this greater being and know that death is not something separate that I must try to figure out, but my own self, as impossible to see with my daylight eyes as the back of my head, but just as rightfully a part of me, and just as highly to be valued. Sylvia tried to tell me this, I think, in her last message, and I will take her word for it, though I have not yet died enough to really understand.

19

Zen Practice:
The Path That Leads to the Extinction of Suffering

■

In the months after Sylvia died, the air turned solid with pain. I could not breathe without taking it in, I couldn't move without feeling it brush against me. It was thickest at home, in the evenings. I sat on the couch with no one opposite me in the striped chair, and looked at the sky through the window above the piano. Twilight was always falling; the sky was always a dead white or a deep hollow gray, and the TV aerials on the rooftops poked up into it desolately, thin and cold. Everything in the house was a word speaking to me about Sylvia. Her handwriting looked up at me from the calendar, where she had marked all the days when the gas man would come to read the meter and I must remember to open the gate. Her clothes hung in her closet, each shirt and shoe speaking of her shape. Her room reeked of the incense we had burned in the last three days, the incense I never wanted to smell again. I put a pan of baking soda in there to absorb it, and then I closed the door.

This is what pain feels like: a fist in the solar plexus. First it hits, and then instead of withdrawing it stays there, pressing and turning. I tried to back away from it, but its arm just became longer and longer, and the fist stayed with me. I could see it coming at the end of the day. It was waiting for me at the table with one placemat, in the hall with the closed door at the end.

Buddhism, says the fourth noble truth, is the path that leads to the extinction of suffering. I wanted to run down that path and get to the place where suffering ceases.

But the path that leads to the extinction of suffering is one of those backward paths like the ones in Alice's looking-glass garden, where the course that seems the most natural and logical is the one that leads you astray. Alice determines to walk to the top of the hill at the end of the garden. She starts up the path with the hill ahead of her, but after a few steps she finds that she is inexplicably walking the other way, with the hill at her back. She takes another path that heads toward the hill, and the same thing happens. All the paths that look as though they'll take her where she wants to go instead perversely shunt her in the opposite direction. Finally she turns and walks away from the hill, and that's when she suddenly finds herself at the top.

It seems to work like this with suffering. You can't walk away from pain in the hope of escaping it; you have to turn around and walk toward it. You have to suffer, as the Guide says, to end suffering. Zen practice is not a way to slip out from under suffering or to numb yourself to it. Quite the contrary. If your practice isn't hard, she says, if it doesn't bring you up against all the things you want least to deal with, if it doesn't require from you great suffering, then you are not really doing spiritual practice. But there is a difference between the suffering that ends suffering and the suffering that perpetuates it. You can learn to distinguish one from the other, and you can, if you are willing to, choose between them.

Night after night in those hard months, I came home hoping I could find a way through the hours of the evening that would take me around the pain instead of through it. But the pain would not be avoided, it was too big. No drink could drown it. No TV show or telephone conversation could silence it. My efforts to stop it had no effect but to darken it with failure.

The more I shrank from pain, the more it crept up behind me like a wave, tugging at my ankles, threatening to pull me off my feet. At last I found that the only way to keep it from swamping me was to do what seemed most perilous — turn to face it. I didn't want to. I would rather have done almost anything else. Nothing else worked.

Writing was my means of confrontation. When all my efforts to fend off the pain had failed and I began to sink, I would force myself to my feet and move across the living room, through fierce currents of resistance, to where the computer stood on its table next to the couch. Heart full of dread, I would flick the switch and plunge in.

The pain streamed through me, out my fingers and onto the screen. Pain was what I wrote about, over and over and over. I looked at it from every angle, described it in all its guises. "It is a dagger," I wrote, "that drives down behind my ribs." "It settles in my solar plexus like a stone and makes my arms limp." "It's as if a hole has been punched out of my middle and the surroundings implode to fill the vacuum, the way air rushes in to fill the vacuum made by a lightning bolt, only in me the result is tears, not thunder." Pain became my familiar — not my friend, but someone whose face I knew. By writing I opened the door to it, I said, "Come in. Run through me." I would write and cry, write and shake, and when I was finished I felt battered but somehow saved.

Months went by, months of this, and although I did not realize for a long time that the pain was ebbing — you can only see that from a great distance, it happens so gradually and with so many backward steps — I *did* notice a change. I began to see that some pain came unavoidably upon me and some I made up myself. The true pain was a sensation, those stabbings and hard blows and aching constrictions. But there was something else as well — a swirling multitude of words that surrounded the pain like a fog. I anguished over what I had done wrong, raged at the past for being how it was instead of how it should have been, recalled words I wished not to have spoken and deeds I wished I had done — as if by denouncing the past, revising it, refusing it, I could repair the unbearable injustice. I knew, in another part of my mind, that this is the way the world is, and worse than this. All I got by fighting it was two pains instead of one: the pain of death and loss and my changed life, and also the pain of my own furious *no!*, my fists balled up, fingernails cutting into my palms. This was extra, added on to the pain. It seemed to happen of itself, and yet I could see, if I looked hard enough, that I didn't *have* to do it.

And here I came upon an unwelcome insight: I was forced to admit that sometimes — often, maybe — I *wanted* to thrash around in my suffering. I didn't want to let the pain go once it had coursed through me, I wanted to hold on to it and recreate it again and again. Something in me was trying to appropriate the pain for its own uses — turn it into a badge I could wear proudly ("Look how I have suffered, much more than you have — I require special treatment"), or maintain me in a broken and helpless condition ("Suffering has ruined my life, not much can be expected from me"). I could feel the terrible seductive sweetness of my pain, the temptation to transform it into something that served my ego and then hang on to it — which is not at all the same as accepting it.

Acceptance is hard. To accept my pain means holding it in my arms, like a package handed to me, my proper burden to be carried. The package may be heavy as lead, or burning hot, or stuck through with razors, but I must concede that it is my package, simply because it has arrived in my life. It is not a mistake. It has not been sent by accident to the wrong person. I may not welcome it, but accepting it means I carry it without protest for as long as necessary — and then I lay it down.

And will it make me happy to follow this hard prescription? I want a guarantee before I start out. But there *is* no guarantee that will satisfy the one who's asking, because it's my ego who wants to know, and my ego is concerned only with my comfort, my pleasures, my success, my importance. Ego rejects all pain, and warns me against it: watch out, this is going to hurt, better protect yourself, better run. Most often I cave in, and my ego smiles and flicks the reins. Every time I am willing to suffer — every time I can say, All right, let it hurt, I accept it — I have flouted ego's authority and loosened a bit the death-grip it has on me.

And this loosening is the path that leads to the extinction of suffering.

There is no end to suffering for my striving, flailing ego-self. It's ego's nature to suffer, and no wisdom is going to improve its nature any more than you can improve an apple so radically that it becomes an orange. It's only outside the ego that there is any end of suffering in sight. Each of the bricks that pave the path must be a pain accepted: a thwarting of the ego.

No one who has ever tried it says this path is easy. It's only preferable to the alternative, which leads down into fear and endless desperate scrambling and the death of the spirit. Nothing guarantees that if I accept my pain I will be a happy person. This path is not concerned with happiness, in the ordinary sense of the word, but with a higher kind of joy, what Buddhists call a "joyful participation in the sorrows of the world." I have seen people who I suspect have come to feel this — Sylvia, at the end of her life, was one. In them the thick wall of the ego has worn papery thin, and they become luminous as lanterns.

20

The House Complete

The house sat by itself for a long time, unfinished, its door and window holes open to the wind. Dust and leaves blew in. Black widows spun their messy webs under the eaves. A mouse drowned in the toilet. I heard these pieces of news from people who walked up there to take a look. I didn't go myself for many months.

Finally house energy began to stir inside me, like a plant that has been dormant for the winter showing signs of life. June finished making the windows, I bought a pair of French doors, and when these had been put into their spaces, the house was at last a real shelter, not a block of air enclosed by walls and a roof. Greg and Tom did the final details — installed the wood stove, put up the window screens, nailed down the last strips of baseboard and molding. The building inspector came and peered suspiciously around. Clear away the lumber scraps, he said, and screw together the sections of stovepipe, and make sure the earth against the back of the house is at least six inches below the window sill. He left without signing his approval. We cleared away the lumber, put in the screws, leveled the dirt, and when he came back he could find nothing else to complain of. He signed on the line, and the house was cut loose from its last strand of red tape.

I bought a tiny tweedy couch that folded out to make a bed-sized pad on the floor, and one day in October, almost two years after Sylvia died, I went up to spend a night in my house for the first time.

It looked as we had wanted it to — as if it belonged there, as if it had not been built on top of the ground but had risen from under it, like a mushroom. All its colors blended with its surroundings —walls brown like the earth, shingles the mottled gray of oak bark. It was a heavy house, built to last, and its presence completed the hillside. If the ground around it had not still been bare and hard, you would have thought the house had always been there.

I got to work, arranging and polishing. All afternoon I sat on the cool floor, rubbing wax into the tiles until they turned from pale dusty brown to a deep glossy auburn, the color of spice tea. I brought in my furniture — the couch, a desk, a pine cupboard for my clothes, two lamps. I set up the desk, which was the kind that comes in sections in a flat package. I scraped putty off the windows and peeled the label off the stovepipe. I screwed a row of hooks onto the wall and hung from them my coat, my umbrella, and my binoculars.

I had brought a picture of Sylvia with me. It shows her looking out from behind a sheet of canvas that was the temporary door of our hermitage in the days when its walls were made of tarpaper. She is emerging from behind the canvas, looking right at the camera, grinning, holding a couple of fingers up in a wry greeting. I set the picture on the sill of the east window.

Night came, and I plugged in my lamps and filled the house with light. Crickets sang outside; cool air came in through the screens. The house was small in the big darkness; it held me close, like a hand.

When I was tired, I sat on the couch and looked around. Everything I needed was within five steps. On a rack over the kitchen sink were my coffee mug, my water glass, my toothbrush and toothpaste, my towel. On the shelves in the corner of the kitchen were my boxes of tea and chocolate, my orange juice, the cans of Sterno for heating water in the coffeepot. My clothes were in the pine cupboard beside the west window, and my computer, plugged into the sun, sat on the desk beneath the east window. On each of the deep windowsills was a lamp. Through the bathroom door, which was a foot or so away from the end of the couch, I could see the white swan-necked toilet, the shelf with my brush and comb, and the window that looked out on the two pine trees. "May all find simplicity the joyous and practical guide," says one of the Buddhist texts we recite here every morning, and right then I found it so. I could not think of anything else I needed.

At bedtime, I pulled out the seat of my couch and piled on it a futon, two slabs of foam rubber, and two sleeping bags to make a bed that would cushion my bones. I slid myself into the top sleeping bag and lay back. Outside the door the stars shone in the branches of the scrub oak. A night bird went *lululu*, and sometime later I heard coyotes yipping and wailing out in the pasture land.

I awoke to see sunlight coming through the window panes, making bright squares on the foot of my bed. I sat up, and in that moment my eye caught a glimpse of something moving outside. Grabbing my glasses, I struggled to my feet, took two steps to the other side of the room, and looked out. Just beyond the window, an animal stopped in its tracks and looked back at me. It was the size of a small dog, long and low to the ground. It had a triangular face like a fox's, and a thick bushy tail like a raccoon's — but it was not a raccoon and not a fox, and not a dog, either. We locked eyes for a few seconds, both of us frozen, and then it bounded off and disappeared over the woodpile, down the hill to the north.

A greeting from the woods, brief and mysterious. Somewhere in my head was the memory of a picture I'd seen in a book — an animal that looked like this, so unfamiliar that I had never seen one, nor even heard its name spoken. A ringtail, I thought it was called, and later, when I went home and looked it up, I found I was right. The creature on the page of the book was posed nearly the same way as the one outside my window — its body in profile, its face turned toward me. It was a rare animal, the book said, seldom seen. But I had seen one, from no more than ten feet away, on the first morning in my new house. I could not help thinking it must be a housewarming present.

My first thought was that it came from Sylvia, who would know that an encounter with a strange animal would be the finest present I could have. Then I thought perhaps the ringtail *was* Sylvia, transmuted, wearing the body of a ringtail temporarily to see how the house looked now that it was finished, and to see how I was doing. And then I thought maybe it was something less personal than that but still arising out of my presence in that house and all the forces that had brought me there. As wind, when it passes through a small hole, becomes sound, so maybe the current of time and events, when it runs through an electric moment in a place charged with feeling, can become visible, taking a suitable shape.

I suppose there is a possibility that the ringtail's appearance was a coincidence — that this singular animal just happened to be there on the morning of my first awakening, at a moment when my eyes were open and looking in the right direction. But I am disinclined to think that events in the world happen so separately and independently, as if there were no connections threading them together. It seems to me that nothing is unconnected, that in each of the ten thousand things of the world, all ten thousand are present. Look at this house, for instance: it is made not just of dirt, wood, glass, and metal, but also of all the forces and substances that created those materials — crumbled rock and leaf mold, iron ore and the fire that forged the steel, sand that melted into glass, waves that ground stones into sand, trees felled and split to make lumber. When you think of it this way, suddenly you see through the materials of the house back down through time and out through space. You realize it's not even just the earth and trees and sand that have made this house, but also the hammer that drove in the nails, and the people who worked in the factories that made the hammer and made the nails. Just as surely, the house is made of the lives of the people who worked on it — Greg, Tom, and June, Sylvia and me and the Guide — and it would not have been itself, not quite the same place, if we were not who we are, which must take into account the parents who brought us into the world, the towns we've lived in, the books we've read, the oatmeal we ate for breakfast, and the farmers who grew the oats. The pink placemats Sylvia and I drew plans on are in this house, and the plans themselves, and all the words that flew in the air between us. Her cancer is in it, and my grief. Look far enough, and you see lines radiating from every particle of the house outward in all directions. All the forces of the universe are combined here, as they are in everything.

A few months later, at the tail end of winter, I burned the brush that we had cut three years before. All that time, it had been standing in piles at the edges of the clearing, gradually drying out, turning a darker brown, splintering and settling. I dragged every branch and stump from the edge to the middle of the clearing, making a mountain of dead wood, and on a rainy morning in March Greg and I took a few branches from the heap, poured kerosene on them, and set them alight. Orange tongues wrapped around the twigs. We added sticks. The flames grew. Before long, flame was rushing up in a sheet, tearing at the tangle of twigs as if trying to escape.

All day I stood by the fire and tossed on branches. Phyl came for a while, and we took the chainsaw to the fallen trees that were too heavy to pull, and to the tree limbs that had broken under last winter's load of snow and hung dying from the trees. Round yellow leaves still clung to these branches, and in the fire they popped and cackled like water hitting grease in a skillet.

At midafternoon, we drank hot chocolate. It was not really a cold day; we didn't have to huddle close to the fire to stay warm. In fact we took our coats off and tossed them on the hood of the car. It is hard work hefting the chainsaw and heaving chunks of wood from here to there. It's hot work, standing by the fire, pushing the sticks in toward the center with a rake, dodging away when the wind blows smoke and flame in your direction. The hot chocolate was not really necessary, except that it felt like keeping a promise. We will burn the brush and drink hot chocolate, Sylvia and I had said, and this was as close as I could get to making that true.

By evening the pile of brush was almost gone. I went down to dinner, and when I came back darkness had fallen, and the heap of coals glowed like the pit of a volcano. I threw on the last branches and sat in the folding chair to watch them burn. Sparks zipped up into the air, zigzagged frantically, dwindled, dropped, and blinked out. The fire hissed like water running fast through a chute. Smoke blew in a plume this way and that, grabbed and turned by the wind. Sometimes a strong gust flattened the flames near to extinction, made the smoke level out and hug close to the ground, made the coals glow fiercely bright.

Clouds rolled over the stars, and scatterings of rain brushed my face. I folded up the chair and went inside to bed. From my pad on the floor I could look out the glass panes of the French doors and see the glow of the fire in the dark. The orange spot brightened and swelled when the wind blew, and then shrank again. A flame wavered up, flickered for a while, went out. I closed my eyes and slept. Sometime in the night, the rain began again, a downpour this time. I heard it on the roof, and I heard the wind rushing in the trees. Rain came down hard hour after hour. By morning, the fire was out.

This marked the end, in my mind, of the time of the house building. It had not worked out the way it was supposed to. Only a little of what we had planned came true, and that in a way we had not intended. This is the nature of plans. Some of them are in harmony with what life has in mind for you, and some are not. I easily forget this and begin to count on the outcome I want as if I had been promised it as a reward for hard work. Then I feel betrayed by life's disdain for my goals. I try to remind myself that we are never promised anything, and that what control we can exert is not over the events that befall us but how we address ourselves to them. I can say, No, this isn't what I wanted, this is not how it was supposed to be, my life has taken a wrong turn. Or I can say, Yes, I see. This is my life. It is being revealed to me, little by little. It could not be other than it is. The threads of it are connected everywhere, they extend into the far reaches of time and space, and they are winding together in a design that is far more rich and wondrous than the one I had in mind for myself.

21

Back to Silence

■

Where the old army tent used to be, a new building is rising, made of rammed earth, like my little house. The earth slabs, roofless so far, stand up against the sky like the stones of Stonehenge, only much neater and straighter. Greg, who learned about rammed earth from helping with my house, is leading the construction, with the monks for his crew. They are doing it by themselves, two men and three women, with occasional weekend help from the rest of us, so the building is going up slowly. When it is finished, it will be dedicated to Sylvia.

I go and help with construction for a few days now and then, sometimes for a few weeks. For me there is more silence at Middlefield than there used to be, even though the building site has been designated a talking area. There is silence on the roads and paths, silence in the screened-in meditation hall in the upper meadow, and silence — unless I talk to myself — in my house.

Strangely enough, it is rarely a lonely silence. Sometimes I even find it hard to tell whether the silence is out there among the oak trees or has somehow gotten inside me. Once, in meditation, I had a strange experience: my head seemed to open like two halves of a clamshell, or like the petals of a flower spreading out. Everything fit into it, all the sounds that were happening outside, and all the space. My familiar talking self shrank to a nut-sized kernel way at the bottom; it was just present enough to say, *Ah!* and take note. I felt nothing but air where my skull had been.

When I thought about this later, I remembered a dream that I had often had in my childhood. I am underwater, holding my breath, coming to the point where my lungs are bursting, and then I remember something I've known for a thousand lifetimes and forgotten — that I can breathe underwater. Of course! There's nothing to it, the trick is only in remembering, and in taking that first breath, which feels like dying. I open my mouth, and the water flows in and fills all the space inside me, so that inside and outside is one substance, no difference. I am a shell that the water streams through.

It was a glimpse, that's all, but it helped me understand something about the rackety rumpus room of my mind. I had thought my task was to improve conditions in there by getting rid of the noise and settling the fights. Now I see it another way: if I stop struggling and turn my back on all the clamor, though this feels like inviting catastrophe, I realize that what I had thought was the whole world is just a small room encompassed by a vast space — and I have been so distracted by the chattering voices that I've failed to notice the room has no walls.

ABOUT THE AUTHOR

Jeanne DuPrau lives in the San Francisco Bay area. She is a graduate of Scripps College in Claremont, California, and a former training and documentation writer for a computer manufacturer. She has been practicing Zen meditation for seven years. This is her third book.